Cambridge Elements

Elements in American Politics
edited by
Frances E. Lee
Princeton University

CONGRESSIONAL EXPECTATIONS OF PRESIDENTIAL SELF-RESTRAINT

Jack B. Greenberg
Yale University

John A. Dearborn
Vanderbilt University

Shaftesbury Road, Cambridge CB2 8EA, United Kingdom

One Liberty Plaza, 20th Floor, New York, NY 10006, USA

477 Williamstown Road, Port Melbourne, VIC 3207, Australia

314–321, 3rd Floor, Plot 3, Splendor Forum, Jasola District Centre, New Delhi – 110025, India

103 Penang Road, #05–06/07, Visioncrest Commercial, Singapore 238467

Cambridge University Press is part of Cambridge University Press & Assessment, a department of the University of Cambridge.

We share the University's mission to contribute to society through the pursuit of education, learning and research at the highest international levels of excellence.

www.cambridge.org
Information on this title: www.cambridge.org/9781009568975

DOI: 10.1017/9781009568968

© Jack B. Greenberg and John A. Dearborn 2025

This publication is in copyright. Subject to statutory exception and to the provisions of relevant collective licensing agreements, no reproduction of any part may take place without the written permission of Cambridge University Press & Assessment.

When citing this work, please include a reference to the DOI 10.1017/9781009568968

First published 2025

A catalogue record for this publication is available from the British Library

ISBN 978-1-009-56897-5 Hardback
ISBN 978-1-009-56895-1 Paperback
ISSN 2515-1606 (online)
ISSN 2515-1592 (print)

Cambridge University Press & Assessment has no responsibility for the persistence or accuracy of URLs for external or third-party internet websites referred to in this publication and does not guarantee that any content on such websites is, or will remain, accurate or appropriate.

For EU product safety concerns, contact us at Calle de José Abascal, 56, 1°, 28003 Madrid, Spain, or email eugpsr@cambridge.org

Congressional Expectations of Presidential Self-Restraint

Elements in American Politics

DOI: 10.1017/9781009568968
First published online: April 2025

Jack B. Greenberg
Yale University

John A. Dearborn
Vanderbilt University

Author for correspondence: Jack B. Greenberg, jack.greenberg@yale.edu

Abstract: This Element explores how Congress has designed laws reliant on an assumption of presidential self-restraint, an expectation that presidents would respect statutory goals by declining to use their formal powers in ways that were legally permissible but contrary to stated congressional intent. Examining several laws addressing political appointments since the 1970s – statutes involving the FBI director, Office of Personnel Management director, chairman of the Joint Chiefs of Staff, director of national intelligence, Federal Emergency Management Agency administrator, inspectors general, Senior Executive Service, vacancies, Social Security Administration commissioner, and Consumer Financial Protection Bureau director – the authors demonstrate lawmakers' reliance on presidential self-restraint in statutory design and identify a variety of institutional tools used to signal those expectations. Furthermore, the authors identify a developmental dilemma: the combined rise of polarization, presidentialism, and constitutional formalism threatens to leave Congress more dependent on presidential self-restraint, even as that norm's reliability is increasingly questionable.

Keywords: Congress, presidency, self-restraint, appointments, separation of powers

© Jack B. Greenberg and John A. Dearborn 2025

ISBNs: 9781009568975 (HB), 9781009568951 (PB), 9781009568968 (OC)
ISSNs: 2515-1606 (online), 2515-1592 (print)

Contents

1 Introduction   1

2 Fixed Terms   8

3 Qualifications   18

4 Removal Reporting Requirements   33

5 Caps   40

6 Removal Protections   47

7 Conclusion   55

    References   67

1 Introduction

In the wake of President Donald Trump's first administration, many members of Congress expressed a desire to push back on what they viewed as his abuses of presidential power during his term in office. To that end, Democrats in the House of Representatives proposed the Protecting Our Democracy Act (PODA), a comprehensive bill responding to many of the actions of the prior Republican president. For example, reacting to Trump's firings of various inspectors general (IGs), the law sought to provide stronger removal protections for those officers. It sought to prevent an IG from being removed as "political retaliation," only allowing an IG to be removed "for a limited number of causes," and requiring the president to "provide Congress with documentation of the cause" in advance of any removal. Likewise, lawmakers also included proposed reforms to "promote filling vacancies with qualified acting officials, incentivize the President to nominate officials for vacancies more rapidly, and close loopholes in existing law."[1] While the bill passed the House, supported by all Democrats and one Republican, it did not pass the Senate, though some provisions of it were later enacted within other legislation.[2]

Still, it was notable that the PODA effort was not merely a response to Trump. In fact, key aspects of the legislation addressed what Congress viewed as limitations of – and deficiencies in – its own prior laws. As bill supporter Representative Peter DeFazio (D-OR) proclaimed, "Anybody who works in the House of Representatives or the Senate should be insulted that you want to empower a president.... This isn't about Donald Trump. It is about the Trump era, which exposed things that need to be fixed, and this law does that."[3] In effect, legislators were acknowledging that presidents had not lived up to prior congressional expectations of *presidential self-restraint* – that they had behaved and utilized their formal powers in ways that were different from what prior legislators had intended.

1.1 Presidential Self-Restraint and the Separation of Powers

This is what we intend to investigate in this Element: the concept of presidential self-restraint in a separation-of-powers system. This idea draws upon a broader notion of "institutional forbearance" posited by Steven Levitsky and Daniel Ziblatt (2018, 106), which they describe as a norm by which "politicians do not

---

[1] "Protecting Our Democracy Act: Section-by-Section," 2021, 12, 17. https://schiff.house.gov/imo/media/doc/PODA%20Section-by-Section%209.16.2021.pdf.
[2] Charlie Savage, "House Approves Post-Trump Curbs on Presidential Power," *New York Times*, December 9, 2021, www.nytimes.com/2021/12/09/us/politics/presidential-power-trump.html.
[3] *Congressional Record*, 117th Congress, 1st Session (December 9, 2021), H7583.

use their institutional prerogatives to the hilt, even if it is technically legal to do so, for such action could imperil the existing system." Forbearance, they suggest, involves "wisdom and self-restraint." Similarly, in her study of presidential unilateralism, Tara Leigh Grove (2020, 925–929) invokes such a concept, arguing that presidents "self-impose" constraints on their ability to issue directives by having them go through an interagency process. This notion was also invoked by President Joe Biden in response to the *Trump v. United States* (2024) decision, in which the Supreme Court ruled that presidents were immune from prosecution for their "official acts."[4] Decrying the decision as "almost certainly mean[ing] that there are virtually no limits on what a President can do," Biden stated that under this "new principle," the "power of the office will no longer be constrained by the law" or the Court. "The only limits," Biden suggested, "will be self-imposed by the President alone."[5] While our research does not focus on potential presidential criminal behavior in carrying out official acts or on presidential unilateral directives, these references to self-imposed constraints on power are suggestive of a key separation-of-powers dynamic that we take up in this Element.

At some level, the notion of one branch of the federal government relying substantially on self-restraint by another branch might seem at odds with classic depictions of the separation of powers. In *Federalist* 51, Publius argued that a system of checks and balances would prevent any one of the three branches of the federal government from dominating the others. Because "ambition must be made to counteract ambition," the Constitution, it was said, gave each branch incentives to defend its own prerogatives: "The interest of the man must be connected with the constitutional rights of the place."[6] Yet, as many statutes remind us, Congress has often passed laws granting significant authority and discretion to the executive branch.[7]

Existing work on separation-of-powers dynamics has uncovered varying and competing logics as to why the legislature exhibits apparent deference to the president rather than attempting to control policy outcomes more directly. These arguments can be grouped into a few general classes. First, some accounts discuss how Congress is unwilling to assert more control, either from a place of torpidity (Fisher 2013), reelection incentives (Fiorina 1982; Schoenbrod 1993; Devins 2009), or partisan interests (Epstein & O'Halloran 1999; Levinson &

---

[4] *Trump v. United States*, 603 U.S. __ (2024) (slip op., 6) (Roberts, C. J., opinion of the Court).
[5] Joseph R. Biden, "Remarks on the United States Supreme Court Ruling on Presidential Immunity," July 1, 2024, *The American Presidency Project*, www.presidency.ucsb.edu/documents/remarks-the-united-states-supreme-court-ruling-presidential-immunity.
[6] James Madison, "The Federalist No. 51" [February 6, 1788], in Ball (2003, 252).
[7] For one account of such laws, see Dearborn (2021, part I).

Pildes 2006; Devins 2009). According to these explanations, Congress is best served offering expansive grants of power to the executive on a wide range of policy matters and focusing its time and resources on more "lucrative" tasks.

Other accounts shed light on how Congress may have difficulties allocating authority in a more judicious manner. Legislators face challenges in directing the bureaucracy, dealing with presidents who "have strong political incentives to bring the federal bureaucracy under their control" (Moe 1989, 328) and "often find[ing] itself in the unenviable position of trying to control bureaucrats for which it has little responsibility for hiring and firing" (McCarty 2004, 413). Moreover, public opinion can potentially constrain Congress from checking the president's powers, such as in times of national security crisis (Lindsay 2003). Even if public opinion were not an obstacle, though, Congress requires sufficient resources to challenge the president in a meaningful way (LaPira, Drutman, & Kosar 2020; Bolton & Thrower 2022). In the absence of that capacity, the promise of ambition counteracting ambition holds little merit.

A third set of arguments discusses the potential societal optimality of the balance of power between the legislature and the executive. What may appear as undue deference to the president by Congress could be an investment in better policy outcomes, possibly even in line with Congress's preferences (Wiseman 2009). It could be lawmakers trying to incentivize presidents to take advantage of bureaucratic expertise by giving them more control over agencies (Gailmard & Patty 2013, ch. 6). Or it could be reflective of a genuine assumption that the president is the rightful custodian of certain powers due to his or her purported unique national perspective (Dearborn 2021). Per these accounts, stricter delegation of power to the president is in some sense unnecessary; the authority Congress grants to the executive is the "right" outcome.

We aim to add to these important accounts by exploring another fundamental separation-of-powers dynamic: the extent to which Congress actively or passively has relied on presidential self-restraint as part of its design of key statutes affecting presidential power. This work builds upon scholarship that has highlighted the ways in which Congress seeks to establish norms about executive branch behavior (Farrar-Myers 2007; Azari & Smith 2012; Renan 2018; Skowronek, Dearborn, & King 2021; Ahmed 2022), such as congressional committees stating expectations in their reports for agencies to follow (Bolton & Thrower 2022, 23). It likewise follows from work that points to the significance of the assumptions about governance and the political environment that lawmakers rely on when designing legislation and the implications of whether those assumptions hold up over time (Dearborn 2021; Devins & Lewis 2023).

In this Element, we ask two questions about Congress's expectations of presidential self-restraint in legislation that addresses political appointments.

First, to what extent and through what institutional devices has Congress expressed expectations of presidential self-restraint in statutes addressing political appointments? By self-restraint, we mean the notion that presidents would avoid using their formal powers in legally permissible ways that would nonetheless circumvent legislative goals. To be sure, we are not arguing that lawmakers *only* resorted to hoping the president would not use power they acknowledged he possessed. Legislators often anticipated that a president would pay political costs for violating this norm. But as our case studies will show, legislators' hopes that the president would choose not to take an action out of fear of it being politically costly were bound together with an expectation of self-restraint. They acknowledged that the president possessed authority that they nonetheless hoped he would not use to violate the spirit of the law; they recognized that presidential self-restraint was required to fully realize the goals of a statute.

Our case studies touch on a variety of institutional tools that Congress can use to bolster – or potentially even reduce its reliance on – the norm of presidential self-restraint in appointments legislation. As David Lewis (2003, 46–48) explains, Congress utilizes such tools in efforts to insulate particular officials and agencies. On the weaker end of the spectrum, Congress could hypothetically grant the president a power but say nothing about its intentions for how the chief executive would use it. Alternatively, legislators might at least suggest a norm by stating what they hoped the president would or would not do.

Other devices would be stronger by serving as institutional expressions of legislators' intent and by setting up identifiable lines that they are expecting the president not to cross. These types of devices simultaneously establish this expectation of self-restraint and set up ways to indicate to the broader political system if a norm violation by the president has occurred. An illustrative example is a provision for a fixed term for an appointee (without removal protections), which would indicate a position is apolitical and that the officeholder should be fired only in unusual circumstances. Here, lawmakers would likely expect the president to pay a political cost for prematurely firing such an official, and they might even anticipate the Senate would decline to confirm the president's preferred replacement nominee as punishment. However, the expectation of self-restraint is fundamental to this arrangement, as lawmakers are relying on the president to refrain from firing that official in the first place and assuming the president will care about the potential political costs of doing so.

A similar dynamic is present in other institutional devices. Removal reporting requirements would not stop a president from firing an official, but they would indicate that such an outcome should be infrequent. Qualifications requirements – which can vary in strength – would be used by Congress to guide the president to choose an officeholder appropriately experienced and prepared for the position. The location of an officer (such as whether or not they are part of the president's Cabinet or are placed in the Executive Office of the President) could be an indication of whether they are supposed to be relatively insulated from political pressure. Congress could also use caps (such as limitations on the number of political appointees a president could install or how long an acting official could serve) as devices to offer the president some flexibility in appointments within defined bounds.

Finally, in contrast to these devices, Congress could attempt to move away from its reliance on self-restraint. At the strong end of the spectrum of the legislature's ability to restrict the president's authority over appointments, lawmakers could specify that certain appointees have for-cause removal protections. Such provisions are meant to formally restrict the president from firing an official at will.

Second, we ask: how have Congress's expectations of presidential self-restraint fared over time? In particular, we pay attention to interrelated developmental trends and their impact on the norm of self-restraint. We show that a combination of rising political polarization and presidentialism has undermined some of the ways in which lawmakers expected a president to pay political costs for using their formal powers in a manner that was legally permissible but at odds with the stated intent of particular statutes. Given this reduced likelihood of a president paying significant political costs, most of the laws we discuss in this Element – which already relied on self-restraint – have become even more dependent on it. Furthermore, we point out the significance of the Supreme Court's turn to constitutional formalism, which has become increasingly evident in recent separation-of-powers cases. This jurisprudential trend threatens to leave Congress fewer institutional options in legislation addressing presidential appointments. The overall result is a developmental dilemma in which lawmakers are left more dependent than ever on the norm of self-restraint, even as its reliability is increasingly called into question.

1.2 Method and Evidence

In this Element, we employ a combination of case studies and process tracing to highlight the centrality of presidential self-restraint in key laws affecting presidential power over appointments since the 1970s.

We have selected laws concerning appointments for several reasons. The appointment power has been one of the most important and enduring subjects of separation-of-powers struggles between the legislature and presidents over time (Lewis 2003, 2008; McCarty 2004; Calabresi & Yoo 2008; Alvis, Bailey, &

Taylor 2013; Katz & Rosenblum 2023). Moreover, the statutes we examine are comparable in terms of time and subject (Gerring 2007). First, these laws were passed in a relatively common context. Since the 1970s, Congress, as a whole, has tended to be more skeptical of an idea that had influenced its disposition toward presidential power in the first half of the twentieth century: the claim that presidents could be counted on to represent the national interest (Dearborn 2021). Second, the laws we analyze addressed relatively similar concerns; Congress was preoccupied with protecting the independence of and promoting the competence of key appointees. Thus, we are not exploring cases in which Congress was simply seeking to delegate authority to the president without restriction. We look at cases in which Congress grappled with how to accomplish certain policy and performance goals while maintaining the relative independence of these officials. Examining such cases should inform our understanding of how reliant Congress may inherently be on presidential self-restraint and how that reliance is changing over time.

The laws we examine are Section 203 of the Crime Control Act of 1976 (establishing a ten-year term for the Federal Bureau of Investigation [FBI] director), the Civil Service Reform Act of 1978 (establishing the Office of Personnel Management [OPM] and Senior Executive Service [SES]), the Goldwater-Nichols Department of Defense Reorganization Act of 1986 (establishing nomination qualifications for the Joint Chiefs of Staff [JCS] chairman) and subsequent 2016 amendments in the National Defense Authorization Act for Fiscal Year 2017, the Intelligence Reform and Terrorism Prevention Act of 2004 (establishing the director of national intelligence [DNI]), the Post-Katrina Emergency Preparedness Act of 2006 (establishing qualifications for the Federal Emergency Management Agency [FEMA] administrator), the Inspector General Act of 1978 and Inspector General Reform Act of 2008 (establishing and then reforming inspector general [IG] appointment and removal procedures), the Federal Vacancies Reform Act of 1998 (setting out revised rules about vacancies and the use of acting officials), the Social Security Program and Improvements Act of 1994 (establishing a single commissioner for the Social Security Administration [SSA], appointed to a six-year term and given for-cause removal protections), and the Dodd-Frank Wall Street Reform and Consumer Protection Act of 2010 (creating the Consumer Financial Protection Bureau [CFPB] with a single director appointed to a five-year term and given for-cause removal protections).

Our analysis of these laws shows that Congress was concerned with promoting the independence of officials within the executive branch. But lawmakers often settled on self-restraint to address a couple of possible concerns. A primary, recurrent issue was the tension between protecting the independence of administrative officials while ensuring those officials could be held accountable for their performance. Additionally, questions or doubts over the constitutionality of potentially stronger institutional constraints on the president often arose. It is important to note, however, that the Supreme Court's jurisprudence on separation-of-powers issues had not yet become as manifestly formalistic as it is today. Lawmakers often explored – and sometimes chose – institutional designs that were subject to constitutional debate in prior decades, but which the judiciary has looked on with greater skepticism more recently.

1.3 Plan of the Element

This Element proceeds by examining statutes involving the FBI director, OPM director, JCS chairman, DNI, FEMA administrator, IGs, SES, vacancies, SSA commissioner, and CFPB director. The cases are organized to highlight institutional devices connected to expectations about presidential conduct, including fixed terms, qualifications, removal reporting requirements, caps, and for-cause removal protections. In some cases, the laws examined here feature multiple such devices. We analyze the legislative histories of these statutes, focusing especially on congressional hearings and floor debates. One concern with this approach would be the potential presence of strategic rhetoric on the part of members of Congress, masking what lawmakers truly thought about the purpose or design of particular legislation. However, we are confident in this approach because we show that the expectations discussed by lawmakers in many of these cases were repeatedly expressed in hearings and floor debates, were widely shared (typically by legislators from both parties), and were directly associated with the design of the legislation.

After demonstrating how Congress expressed expectations that presidents would avoid using their formal powers in contravention of the goals of these statutes, we suggest developmental implications involving the combined rise of presidentialism, polarization, and constitutional formalism. In addition to noting connections between rising political polarization and broader trends in presidential power over the last few decades, we focus on direct violations of the congressional expectations of presidential self-restraint. Concurrently, we discuss how the polarized political climate dims prospects for bipartisan institutional reforms that would address violations of Congress's expectations for presidential behavior, such as the PODA legislation.

Furthermore, we explain the implications of the ascent of constitutional formalism in recent decades. We describe how the Supreme Court has embraced a formalistic reading of the separation of powers. Its conservative majority has adopted key tenets of the unitary executive theory, whose advocates argue that the president possesses "*all* of the executive power" under Article II of the Constitution.[8] We point to how this vision of the separation of powers curtails Congress's ability to insulate executive branch positions from direct presidential control. Ultimately, constitutional formalism risks leaving legislators with little recourse aside from presidential self-restraint at a time when executive virtue is far from the most reliable of forces.

2 Fixed Terms

2.1 Federal Bureau of Investigation Director

An early example of Congress legislating its expectations for presidential self-restraint in the post-Watergate era was Section 203 of the Crime Control Act of 1976. This section established a single ten-year term for the FBI director but left the position subject to at-will removal by the president. Throughout the debates over these changes, lawmakers emphasized the significance of the FBI's independence. Because of "the great value of the FBI as a criminal investigative agency, as well as its dangerous potential for infringing individual rights and serving partisan or personal ambitions," a report on the Senate legislation stated, the "office of FBI Director [was] unique." Correspondingly, Congress needed to exercise "the greatest care... in creating an environment for the responsible use of power."[9]

In considering reform, lawmakers aimed to respond to what they viewed as recent abuses of presidential power over the FBI, particularly during the administration of Republican President Richard Nixon. Senator Robert Byrd (D-WV) argued that "the politicization of the Bureau, while always a threat in the past, became a reality" during Nixon's presidency. In his view, the FBI had become "an arm of the administration in its campaign for reelection, and subsequent efforts to suppress the truth behind the sordid background of that campaign." As a result, lawmakers selected an institutional device meant to buttress the expectation that the president would restrain himself from interfering in FBI investigative matters and from putting political pressure on the director (Renan 2018, 2210). A ten-year fixed term, Byrd asserted, would mean that "the Director can be more effectively insulated from political pressures liable to be placed on him by a President, and he will not be considered a politically oriented member of the President's 'team.'"[10] FBI Director

---

[8] *Morrison v. Olson*, 487 U.S. 654, 705 (1988) (Scalia, J., dissenting). Emphasis in original.
[9] *Ten-Year Term for FBI Director*, Report to accompany S. 2106, United States Senate, 93rd Congress, 2nd Session (Washington, DC: Government Printing Office, 1974), 2–3.
[10] *Ten-Year Term for FBI Director*, Hearing before the Subcommittee on FBI Oversight of the Committee on the Judiciary, United States Senate, 93rd Congress, 2nd Session (Washington, DC: Government Printing Office, 1974), 1.

Clarence Kelley agreed that a ten-year term "might contribute toward countering the impression that an appointment of any Director was for political purposes." Moreover, Kelley suggested that "the position of Director should not necessarily change hands with each administration," providing the officeholder with "a greater sense of independence."[11]

The problem, as lawmakers saw it, was that Congress had not previously clarified its expectations for the position explicitly in statute. As a Senate report on the proposal stated, "Congress has expressed no desire that the President consider any period of time as an appropriate length of service for a Director." "In the absence of Congressional guidance," the report declared, "a newly elected President may feel free to replace the Director with a nominee of his own choosing, subject to the advice and consent of the Senate, immediately upon taking office." Alternatively, a director might be able to stay in office longer by "satisfy[ing] the wishes" of several "succeeding Presidents."[12] Legislators thus sought to use the ten-year term to bolster a norm of investigatory independence, indicating that the FBI should be free of political pressure from the president that would improperly affect the director in carrying out law enforcement responsibilities.

Still, a complication in Congress's efforts was that legislators were also concerned about balancing independence for the FBI Director with effective accountability. Even as lawmakers were concerned about presidential pressure on the director, they also feared a director serving as long as J. Edgar Hoover had. In their view, Hoover's long service led to him acquiring too much autonomy and becoming politically untouchable (Gage 2022). The two goals of reform rested uneasily alongside each other, notwithstanding legislators' assertions that they fit well together. As one Senate report had put it, "The purpose of the bill is to achieve two complementary objectives." The first goal was "to insulate the Director of the Federal Bureau of Investigation from undue pressure being exerted upon him from superiors in the Executive Branch." Lawmakers wanted to provide "independence from any reasonable or unjustifiable requests made by the Director's superiors," and the ten-year term was viewed as giving "the Director some degree of protection from dismissal without good reason." The second goal was "to protect against an FBI Director becoming too independent and unresponsive." Legislators saw a "legitimate concern that a Director might build up so much power through long service that he would become, in effect, politically unremovable by the President."[13]

Lawmakers intended the ten-year term to indicate that the president would pay a political cost for prematurely dismissing the director. "As a practical

---

[11] Ibid., 4. [12] *Ten-Year Term for FBI Director*, Report, 2. [13] Ibid., 1.

matter," the ten-year term was thought to "preclude a President from arbitrarily naming a new FBI Director without showing good reasons for dismissal of his predecessor." An unjustified firing, the Senate report stressed, would mean that "the chances for confirmation by the Senate of a new nominee would be remote." Thus, the legislation functioned as "a cautionary message to the President to the effect that whereas his power to remove a Director of the FBI is formally unlimited, nevertheless, by virtue of its power to ratify the appointment of a successor, the Senate retains a large measure of influence over this removal power and will tolerate its exercise for good reason only." The president "would be expected to justify the mid-term removal of an FBI Director... and not merely for the reason that a new President desires his 'own man' in the position."[14] Senator Byrd stated that the law would "make it clear that the Congress does not want any President to use the seat of the FBI Director as he may those of his Cabinet officers, in playing games of musical chairs."[15] "I suppose that under practically any system, were you to speculate about what might happen under certain conditions, you could raise some critical issues," admitted FBI Director Kelley. But he was "confident that when the Senate confirms an FBI Director, its Members will have done their work well."[16] The provision "would assure stability," asserted Representative Peter Rodino (D-NJ), and "assures us some degree of control over this office."[17]

Still, even as lawmakers sought to bolster a norm against premature removal by indicating potential political costs to the president, they acknowledged their inherent reliance on presidential self-restraint. The president retained removal authority over the FBI director, but they expected him to decline to use it (Hamlin 2019). As the Senate report stated, "The bill does not place any limit on the formal power of the President to remove an FBI Director from office within the ten-year term. The Director would be subject to dismissal by the President, as are all purely executive officers."[18] Byrd emphasized that "the FBI Director is a highly placed figure in the executive branch and he can be removed by the President at any time, and for any reason that the President sees fit."[19] Representative Charles Wiggins (R-CA) pointedly told his House colleagues that the final legislation was "somewhat misleading and perhaps even illusory" because "the President retains the right to discharge" the director "for whatever cause he deems appropriate," even though "he may have been appointed and confirmed by the Senate for a fixed term."[20]

---

[14] Ibid., 6–7.   [15] *Ten-Year Term for FBI Director*, Hearing, 7.   [16] Ibid., 5.
[17] *Congressional Record*, 94th Congress, 2nd Session (September 30, 1976), 34117.
[18] *Ten-Year Term for FBI Director*, Report, 6.
[19] *Ten-Year Term for FBI Director*, Hearing, 7.
[20] *Congressional Record*, 94th Congress, 2nd Session (September 30, 1976), 34117.

Notably, some lawmakers had sought to avoid a reliance on presidential self-restraint with a different institutional solution. In 1973, Senator Henry "Scoop" Jackson (D-WA) and Senator Richard Schweiker (R-PA) each introduced legislation that would have made the FBI independent of the DOJ and provided for-cause removal protections for the director. Jackson sought to use this mechanism to ensure the director was "insulated from Presidential pressure"; likewise, Schweiker looked to keep the director "fully insulated from political pressure."[21] Other lawmakers, though, acknowledged potential constitutional concerns with that approach. The Senate report suggested that it was "highly likely" that the president "may well have illimitable constitutional power to remove an FBI Director, as that office is presently constituted by law." It noted that the FBI was "the investigative arm of the Department of Justice – a Department which is 'an executive department of the United States.'" Crucially, the report asserted there was not a "compelling case" to make the FBI "independent of the Justice Department or for its policies to be removed from the supervision of the Attorney General."[22] Still, this disagreement shows that lawmakers were well aware of different alternative solutions to try to provide the director with more political insulation and that their chosen solution involved a greater reliance on self-restraint by the president.

In the end, for legislation addressing a particularly sensitive political appointment, Congress's approach to balancing accountability and independence was to set an expectation of presidential self-restraint. Moreover, lawmakers' reticence to seek firmer removal protections indicates how concerns over the boundaries of the president's authority under Article II could leave legislators more reliant on norms of self-restraint.

2.2 Office of Personnel Management Director

In debates over the Civil Service Reform Act of 1978, Congress again grappled with concerns over the independence of key officials (Ingraham & Ban 1984; Moynihan 2004). As bill sponsor Senator Abraham Ribicoff (D-CT) put it, lawmakers were dealing with concerns over "providing adequate management flexibility while at the same time assuring that the civil service system and employees are protected against partisan political abuse and arbitrary actions."[23]

---

[21] *Congressional Record*, 93rd Congress, 1st Session (April 6, 1973), 11353; *Congressional Record*, 93rd Congress, 1st Session (May 3, 1973), 14130; Andrew Kent, "Congress Should Reconsider Giving the FBI Director Independence from Presidential Control," *Lawfare*, July 14, 2017, www.lawfaremedia.org/article/congress-should-reconsider-giving-fbi-director-independence-presidential-control.

[22] *Ten-Year Term for FBI Director*, Report, 6.

[23] *Congressional Record*, 95th Congress, 2nd Session (August 24, 1978), 27536.

Democratic President Jimmy Carter had pressed the issue of civil service reform in submitting to Congress his Reorganization Plan No. 2, and lawmakers concurrently crafted legislation responding to that plan.[24] In addition to the creation of the SES, which we discuss in a subsequent section, the legislation made a significant change to the overall management structure of the civil service. The responsibilities of the former Civil Service Commission (CSC) were split between a new OPM, which would handle personnel policies, and a new Merit Systems Protection Board (MSPB) and special counsel to handle federal employee treatment (Moynihan 2004, 4). The different institutional designs Congress chose for the OPM director versus the MSPB and special counsel are instructive for determining the extent to which legislators relied on expectations of presidential self-restraint in dealing with each agency.

Those who advocated a change from a bipartisan three-member CSC to an OPM headed by a single director acknowledged that this would place more direct responsibility on the president for personnel management. Those who viewed this change positively emphasized the significance of accountability and responsibility. The CSC chairman, Alan Campbell, argued in the House hearings on the proposal that the "close relationship" between the proposed OPM director and the president would "emphasize the President's direct responsibility for the personnel system, including responsibility to carry out the merit system laws."[25] Likewise, Elmer Staats, the comptroller general, testified in Senate hearings that the existing CSC was a "form of organization" that "tends to be cumbersome and divides responsibility and accountability."[26]

However, even advocates of the change to a single OPM director acknowledged concerns over the potential closeness of this official to the president. Campbell noted that some had "fear that the Director is too close to Presidential influence and therefore susceptible to political pressure in policymaking." But he expressed confidence that it was "simply unrealistic to believe that the Director willfully may inject political considerations into the personnel rules for the career system." To bolster that assertion, he pointed to both "the merit principles and prohibited practices" being included in the law, and emphasized

---

[24] Jimmy Carter, "Federal Civil Service Reorganization Message to the Congress Transmitting Reorganization Plan No. 2 of 1978," May 23, 1978, *The American Presidency Project*, www.presidency.ucsb.edu/documents/federal-civil-service-reorganization-message-the-congress-transmitting-reorganization-plan.

[25] *Civil Service Reform*, Hearings before the Committee on Post Office and Civil Service, House of Representatives, 95th Congress, 2nd Session (Washington, DC: Government Printing Office, 1978), 125–126.

[26] *Civil Service Reform Act of 1978 and Reorganization Plan No. 2 of 1978*, Hearings before the Committee on Governmental Affairs, United States Senate, 95th Congress, 2nd Session (Washington, DC: Government Printing Office, 1978), 537.

that the MSPB would be "a watchdog."[27] Staats, too, recognized "the concern which has been expressed that a single Director of Personnel, serving at the pleasure of the President and replacing a bipartisan commission, could be accused of partisan political motivations in actions which, by their very nature, are controversial." Senator Charles Percy (R-IL) pressed this point, asking Staats whether the position was sufficiently insulated from political pressure: "Do you feel there is any problem in having the Director of Personnel serve at the pleasure of the President? Would that tend to make it too much a political appointment?" But Staats responded by suggesting that the OPM had a distinct role from other institutions in the legislation, necessitating less formal protection for independence: "I don't really think so. I fully support the idea of having terms of office for the Merit Systems Protection Board. I think the function of the Director of Personnel is different. His role is different."[28]

Still, other legislators and congressional hearing witnesses were concerned about an OPM director so tied to the president. These concerns touched upon whether Congress could trust that the president would exercise self-restraint and not use his influence over the OPM director to manipulate the civil service. An exchange between Senator Charles Mathias (R-MD) and Campbell centered on this point. Thinking through how the design of the OPM might facilitate the politicization of the civil service, Mathias emphasized that "we, of course, are legislating here for more than one administration." Mathias noted that agencies making requests to the CSC to take "positions out of the competitive service" had "been an area of White House activity in the past." For his part, Campbell suggested that "the existence of a special counsel and the Merit Systems Protection Board" meant that there would be "an independent agency that would be able, if such actions were inappropriate, to take corrective action." But Mathias pointed to the vulnerability of the OPM's single director to presidential pressure due to being subject to at-will removal: "it troubles me that in this policymaking area with the director of the Office of Personnel Management, who serves at the pleasure of the President [and] is removable at any time by the President, will be far more vulnerable to pressure from various sources, from the agencies or from White House intervention, which we agree has happened in the past." Mathias further explained that the bipartisan CSC had "been subject to pressure at points in the past," and that such political pressure was inevitable: "there is no way in the world that we can prevent pressure." "Those things are going to occur," stressed Mathias: "And it just seems to me that the position in

---

[27] *Civil Service Reform*, Hearings, 125.
[28] *Civil Service Reform Act of 1978 and Reorganization Plan No. 2 of 1978*, Hearings, 537, 581.

which we are putting the director of the Office of Personnel Management is that he is going to be vulnerable to that practice."[29]

Campbell responded again by suggesting that the virtue of the legislation was placing responsibility directly on the president. He argued that the change from the "quasi-independent" CSC – whose members were subject to at-will removal – would ultimately "place the responsibility where it belongs, on the President, and on the heads of the departments and agencies" and not allow them "to hide behind the Commission." But Mathias was not fully convinced that this was sufficient to prevent political manipulation of the system by the president, making a direct reference to the recent Watergate scandal: "When we are making the effort to restructure the system, we ought to accomplish something more than merely getting access to hindsight. It is all very well to say the President's responsibility will be very clear and that will give an opportunity to some future Woodward and Bernstein to write stories and some future Herblock to draw a cartoon, but it will be after the fact."[30]

These concerns over the OPM's structure were a recurrent theme in the congressional hearings. "The possibilities and probabilities of manipulation for political purposes and personal favoritism are enormous," suggested Gene Raymond, the executive director of the National Federation of Federal Employees, "since the plan calls for a single administrator who serves at the pleasure of the President and is part of the Executive Office of the President, that person will not have the same degree of independence as does the bipartisan body that now oversees the CSC."[31] A former CSC executive director, Bernard Rosen, likewise argued that "the possibilities for manipulating the civil service for personal or political favoritism would be greatly increased because personnel policy would be made by an administrator serving at the pleasure of the President, instead of by a bi-partisan body."[32] Vincent Connery, the national president of the National Treasury Employees Union, expressed concern that the OPM director, "answerable only to the President, would literally become the personnel czar for the entire Federal Government."[33] And the American Nurses Association suggested that OPM's structure "involves grave risks," advocating for an amendment "to provide that the Director of the Office of Personnel Management have fixed tenure and, once appointed by the President and confirmed by the Senate, can be removed only for a good cause."[34]

---

[29] Ibid., 48–50.   [30] Ibid., 51.   [31] Ibid., 665.
[32] *Civil Service Reform*, Hearings, 847.
[33] *Civil Service Reform Act of 1978 and Reorganization Plan No. 2 of 1978*, Hearings, 1306.
[34] *Civil Service Reform*, Hearings, 949.

The potential concerns over the OPM's structure were not discussed in isolation; Congress was also considering the structure of the MSPB and its special counsel in the civil service legislation. From the outset, it was widely agreed that the MSPB would have strong protections for its independence and insulation. As Campbell testified, the MSPB would have members with nonrenewable terms of seven years and who would be removable by the president "only for reasons of misconduct, inefficiency, neglect of duty, or malfeasance."[35] In this way, lawmakers made it clear that they would not rely on the president's good will with the agency.

The MSPB also included a special counsel to act to investigate abuses. Unlike the MSPB members, the special counsel was initially not envisioned as being protected from at-will removal. When asked by Representative Gladys Spellman (D-MD) whether "the purpose of this section" not providing "removal criteria" would be "to give the President the authority to fire the special counsel at will," H. Patrick Swygert, the CSC's general counsel, explained that the administration's "position has been that the President has the authority and the power to discharge the special counsel at will." The administration provided an Office of Legal Counsel (OLC) opinion suggesting constitutional concerns over formal insulation of the special counsel. The OLC acknowledged that the "affiliation" of the special counsel with the "quasi-judicial" MSPB "might arguably be taken to justify a status independent of the President." However, because the special counsel would have "responsibilities which he is to perform without direction from the Board" and would have "a status independent of and apart from the Board," the OLC argued that the position could not be insulated from at-will removal: "Since it is only the quasi-judicial or quasi-legislative nature of an official's duties that justify a measure of independence from Presidential control... there is no justification for according such independence to the Special Counsel here."[36]

Still, despite the administration's position on constitutionality, the issue of special counsel protections was a theme of the congressional hearings. For example, in an exchange with the president of Common Cause, David Cohen, Senator Ribicoff explained that "much has been made of the role of the special counsel who is the primary investigator and the protector of the merit system." "Yet," he went on, the bill under consideration would provide "that he is removable without any showing of cause." When asked by Ribicoff whether "you think the special counsel should be removable only for cause," Cohen responded, "I do." When Ribicoff asked, "shouldn't we require that if he gets removed, there ought to be some real reason given," Cohen agreed that "there

---

[35] Ibid., 125.   [36] Ibid., 819–820.

ought to be some real reasons." Cohen explained that these protections for independence were "important to not only protect against abuses," but would also facilitate the legislation's "system of protection for whistle blowers."[37]

A similar point was made in a written exchange between Ribicoff and the consumer advocate Ralph Nader and lawyer Andrew Feinstein. In response to Ribicoff asking whether "the Special Counsel should be removable only for cause," Nader and Feinstein agreed that "our preference would be for a Special Counsel removable only for cause." While acknowledging that the Carter administration had "suggested that certain constitutional constraints exist on its ability to insulate the Special Counsel from the President's removal power," they did "not subscribe" to that view.[38] In a written position paper, Connery, the national president of the National Treasury Employees Union, similarly raised issues with at-will removal of the special counsel. Since, under the proposal, "the Special Counsel serves at the will of the President and can be removed 'without cause,'" Connery suggested "that serious allegations of impropriety by Federal officials could go untouched, if that is the desire of the White House." Connery invoked Watergate: "An even greater danger is that the President could direct the Special Counsel to use the powers of the office to 'get' employees who are out of political favor. A stalwart individual in the Special Counsel's position who sought to resist such pressure would soon be the victim of another 'Saturday Night Massacre.'"[39]

For a period, it appeared possible there would be no difference in outcome and that Congress would turn away from self-restraint by providing for-cause removal protections for both the OPM director and the special counsel. The Senate bill had included for-cause removal protections to both the director of OPM and the special counsel. As Senator Ribicoff explained, the bill would prevent the president from removing the OPM director "for political reasons, or for any other reason except for cause, that is, inefficiency, neglect of duty, or malfeasance in office." He suggested this provision strengthened the OPM director's insulation from the president compared to the existing CSC commissioners. Since the CSC commissioners "may be removed by the President at any time for any reason," Ribicoff posited, "the Commission is not a safe check against the broad discretionary powers the President has under the civil service laws to issue rules, and direct the management of the civil service system." Likewise, Ribicoff explained that the special counsel would have such protections for insulation under the Senate's preferred legislation. Having "a four-year term," the special counsel "may not be removed by the

---

[37] *Civil Service Reform Act of 1978 and Reorganization Plan No. 2 of 1978*, Hearings, 294–295.
[38] Ibid., 432–433.   [39] Ibid., 1327.

President during the term except for inefficiency, neglect of duty, or malfeasance in office."[40]

However, the House legislation differed on some of these dimensions. The bill similarly provided that the special counsel could face removal "only upon notice and hearing and only for misconduct, inefficiency, neglect of duty, or malfeasance in office." But it contained no language regarding the removal of the OPM director, meaning that the president would have such removal authority.[41] Indeed, the House report on the legislation stressed the OPM's connection to the president, stating it would "serve as the President's agent for all civil service personnel matters." While noting "concern which has been expressed that a single director of personnel, serving at the pleasure of the President and replacing a bipartisan commission, could be accused of partisan political motivations," the House report offered several rationales for this move. It suggested that a commission "divides responsibility and accountability," pointing to President Franklin Roosevelt's 1937 Committee on Administrative Management proposal for a single personnel director, and noted that such a reform had "been extensively adopted at the State and local level." Thus, "on balance," the House report stated a preference for a single director.[42]

The final legislation's distinction between the OPM director and special counsel marked a difference in the extent to which Congress relied on presidential self-restraint. The OPM director was given a four-year term but no longer enjoyed removal protections. As the conference report explained, the compromise "deletes the limitation on the President's removal power contained in the Senate bill, making the Director removable at the will of the President." Still, the report emphasized the need for independence from the president, pointing to the fixed term as a way to encourage the president to exercise self-restraint and not fire the director for political reasons: "In order to provide the Director with a measure of independence from the President in performing his duties, though, the conference substitute provides that the Director have a 4-year term, and deletes the Senate requirement that the term be coterminous with that of the President."[43] As in the case of the FBI director, then, Congress simultaneously raised the possibility of the president paying a political cost for an unjustified premature dismissal of the OPM director, while also acknowledging that they were expecting the chief executive to avoid using authority that he possessed.

---

[40] *Congressional Record*, 95th Congress, 2nd Session (August 24, 1978), 27536.

[41] *Congressional Record*, 95th Congress, 2nd Session (September 13, 1978), 29224–29225.

[42] *Civil Service Reform Act of 1978*, Report of the Committee on Post Office and Civil Service on H.R. 11280 to Reform the Civil Service Laws, House Report No. 95–1403 (Washington, DC: Government Printing Office, 1978), 6.

[43] *Civil Service Reform Act of 1978*, Conference Report to accompany S. 2640, 95th Congress, 2nd Session (Washington, DC: Government Printing Office, 1978), 132.

By contrast, the final legislation relied far less on presidential self-restraint with regard to the special counsel. Despite the constitutional concerns about removal restrictions that had been raised, the law provided the special counsel a five-year term, specified a nomination qualification (that the individual should be an attorney), and gave the position for-cause removal protections: "The Special Counsel of the Merit Systems Protection Board shall be appointed by the President from attorneys, by and with the advice and consent of the Senate, for a term of 5 years.... The Special Counsel may be removed by the President only for inefficiency, neglect of duty, or malfeasance in office."[44] Congress strengthened this position further in the Whistleblower Protection Act of 1989, establishing a distinct Office of Special Counsel (OSC) as a separate federal agency from the MSPB, keeping the removal restrictions, and stipulating an additional qualification that the position be someone "especially qualified to carry out the functions of the position."[45]

3 Qualifications

3.1 Chairman of the Joint Chiefs of Staff

Similar debates over independence arose as Congress considered reforms to the JCS. Legislators wrestled with how to promote independent and professional military counsel while maintaining civilian command. In the Goldwater-Nichols Department of Defense Reorganization Act of 1986, lawmakers settled on a combination of institutional devices – a fixed term and stated qualifications for the position – that aimed to promote the independence of the JCS chairman, while still being reliant on presidential self-restraint.

A series of military failures in the late 1970s and early 1980s – the unsuccessful attempt to rescue American hostages during the Iranian Revolution, the bombing of Marine barracks in Beirut, and poor communication and intelligence gathering ahead of the invasion of Grenada – prompted the legislature to consider how it could improve operational command of the armed forces.[46] Congress wanted to combat interservice rivalries and provide the president with stronger, more holistic military advice. Representative Richard White (D-TX), the chairman of the House Armed Services Committee's Investigations

---

[44] Ibid., 14.
[45] Whistleblower Protection Act of 1989 (PL 101–12, 103 Stat. 16, April 10, 1989). In 1994, Congress further authorized that the special counsel could serve up to one potential extra year until a successor was appointed and qualified.
[46] *Beyond Goldwater-Nichols: U.S. Government and Defense Reform for a New Strategic Era*, Phase 2 Report, Center for Strategic and International Studies, July 28, 2005, 14, www.csis.org/analysis/beyond-goldwater-nichols-phase-ii-report.

Subcommittee, argued that "rebuilding our defenses requires improvement in the way we conduct our military affairs ... We agree with General [Edward] Meyer's assertion that... 'there is a far greater need today for improved military advice.'"[47]

Among other changes, the 1986 law that resulted from this effort designated the JCS chairman as the "principal military adviser" to the president (Zegart 1999, 140–148).[48] The chairman, who would serve a two-year term, was meant to rise above the parochialism of their particular service branch and adopt a broad view of the military's needs and capabilities. The act made clear that the chairman was not in the chain of command; the president or Secretary of Defense would still provide orders to the combatant commanders. Nevertheless, the holistic vantage point that the chairman would offer was deemed essential. Senator George Mitchell (D-ME) stated that this arrangement "promises a solution to the problem created by the present JCS structure, which asks of each Chief that he simultaneously function as an advocate for his service and that he subordinate service interests in favor of some broader perspective."[49]

However, some lawmakers were concerned about the potential of the JCS chairman to foster executive aggrandizement. For example, Representative Ron Dellums (D-CA) emphasized "that it is reasonable to assume that the President will want a Chairman who will represent his particular point of view in the [National Security Council]," an intervention that "could be at the expense of, or contrary to, the military advice he might otherwise be giving."[50] A JCS chairman charged by the president to "do his bidding" would not only undermine the legislature's goal of achieving independent judgment but risk the emergence of "a more politicized military establishment."[51]

But key legislators who supported the reforms argued the legislation would improve the quality of military advice, not undermine civilian control or subject the chairman to undue presidential influence. Representative Ike Skelton (D-MO) contended that the bill would "actually improve civilian control because it ensures the Secretary of Defense and the President of the United States are getting better,

---

[47] *Reorganization Proposals for the Joint Chiefs of Staff*, Hearings before the Investigations Subcommittee of the Committee on Armed Services, House of Representatives, 97th Congress, 2nd Session (Washington, DC: Government Printing Office, 1982), 2.

[48] Goldwater-Nichols Department of Defense Reorganization Act of 1986 (100 Stat. 992, PL 99–433, October 1, 1986).

[49] *Congressional Record*, 99th Congress, 2nd Session (May 7, 1986), 9866.

[50] *Joint Chiefs of Staff Reorganization Act of 1985*, Report to accompany H.R. 3622, 99th Congress, 1st Session, Report 99–375 (Washington, DC: Government Printing Office, 1985), 35.

[51] *Full Committee Consideration of H.R. 3622*, Hearing before the Committee on Armed Services, House of Representatives, 99th Congress, 1st Session (Washington, DC: Government Printing Office, 1987 [1985]), 59; *Joint Chiefs of Staff Reorganization Act of 1985*, Report, 33.

more timely advice on military strategy; hence, they can do a better job of making the right decisions."[52] For Skelton, the purpose was to make the military's advice more holistic and to ensure the president listened to it: "Rather than have watered down pablum type advice to the President, and to the Secretary of Defense, we will have clear, concise, timely advice that a President and Secretary can rely on. In the past there have been Presidents that have either chosen to ignore, or only listen to part of, the advice. They sought their advice elsewhere. We will end that."[53] John Lochner III, the director of a staff study on "Defense Organization: The Need for Change" and a staffer for the Senate Armed Services Committee, emphasized, "We are looking to get the kind of professional military advice to the Secretary of Defense, the President, and the National Security Council that they deserve. They have not gotten it in the past, and on occasion they have disregarded the advice that has been provided. . ... what we are essentially saying is that professional military advice has not played the role that it should in decisionmaking." At the same time, other lawmakers acknowledged that they were ultimately reliant on the president to listen to that advice. Senator John Warner (R-VA), for example, replied to Lochner that "there is no way we can assure that any President is going to follow the advice of the military commanders, I do not care what kind of title or caption you give them."[54]

One of the law's key innovations sought to reduce Congress's reliance on the good intentions of the president. Lawmakers viewed the stated qualifications for the role as a key check on the potential for the president to politicize the chairmanship. Specifically, the statute required the chairman to have previously served as vice chairman of the JCS (a new position created by the act), a service chief (e.g., chief of staff of the Army), or a combatant commander (e.g., commander of Central Command). It likewise required the vice chairman and combatant commanders to have had at least one joint-duty assignment as a general or a flag officer. The Senate Armed Services Committee believed "that previous joint experience would greatly help the Chairman, the Vice Chairman, and the Service Chiefs carry out their JCS duties."[55] While the Senate had an initial preference for requiring joint experience for the JCS chairman, the final legislation resolved a House-Senate discrepancy by also allowing the JCS chairman to have served as a service chief: "The Senate

---

[52] *Reorganization Proposals for the Joint Chiefs of Staff – 1985*, Hearings, 18.
[53] *Full Committee Consideration of H.R. 3622*, Hearing, 44–45.
[54] *Reorganization of the Department of Defense*, Hearings before the Committee on Armed Services, United States Senate, 99th Congress, 1st Session (Washington, DC: Government Printing Office, 1987 [1985]), 32.
[55] *Department of Defense Reorganization Act of 1986*, Report to accompany S. 2295, Committee on Armed Services, United States Senate, 99th Congress, 2nd Session (Washington, DC: Government Printing Office, 1986), 20.

recedes with an amendment to require, subject to a waiver by the President, that the Chairman have served as the Vice Chairman, a Service Chief, or a unified or specified combatant commander before his appointment."[56] Conditional on the chairman only emerging from the top ranks of the military, supportive lawmakers were skeptical of the notion that he would function as a mere agent of the President's agenda. Senator Carl Levin (D-MI) found "it almost inconceivable that a senior officer would alter his fundamental views to curry favor with a President."[57] Skelton declared that he was "not at all concerned" about politicization because "the system just won't allow it."[58]

Still, while the formal experience provision went beyond simply hoping the president would choose qualified individuals, the legislation nonetheless relied on presidential self-restraint. First, the legislation allowed the president to waive the past service stipulation for the posts. As a Senate report put it, this "would preserve the President's flexibility in assigning these senior military officers by authorizing him to waive this requirement if he determines such action to be in the national interest."[59] Thus, lawmakers were depending on the president to avoid waiving that requirement unnecessarily, though of course the Senate would retain the ability to impose a cost on the president by rejecting his nominee.

The conference report's discussion of the professional experience requirements also clarified this understanding of presidential self-restraint. As legislators recognized, affording the president the ability to waive the qualification requirements presented an opportunity for the chief executive to disrupt this arrangement. Congress's expectations about how often the president should use his waiver authority were clearly stated in the context of the vice chairman and the combatant commanders. House and Senate conferees suggested that such waivers should be rare and that the provision was mainly meant to allow time for developing a pipeline of officers with joint experience. Thus, legislators distinguished between temporary and permanent waiver authority. For both the role of the vice chairman and the roles of combatant commander, "the conferees agreed to provide a specific waiver for a limited transition period so that the exercise of a Presidential waiver, as would be required in the immediate future, would not become standard practice. After the transition period, the conferees expect the President to exercise his permanent waiver authority only in an

---

[56] *Goldwater-Nichols Department of Defense Reorganization Act of 1986*, Conference Report to accompany H.R. 3622, 99th Congress, 2nd Session, House of Representatives (Washington, DC: Government Printing Office, 1986), 108.
[57] *Congressional Record*, 99th Congress, 2nd Session (May 7, 1986), 9830.
[58] *Full Committee Consideration of H.R. 3622*, Hearing, 59.
[59] *Department of Defense Reorganization Act of 1986*, Report, 20.

extremely limited number of cases and only for officers of exceptional talent who may fail to meet the specified criteria."[60] Somewhat curiously, the conference report did not dwell on the president's waiver ability in relation to the chairmanship. Notably, one of the ways a JCS chairman could have relevant professional experience was to be a service chief, perhaps lessening the need for the kind of multi-year transition period legislators identified for the vice chairman and combatant commander roles. In any case, it was clear that lawmakers were depending on the president to restrain himself from unnecessarily using the waiver authority.

Second, lawmakers acknowledged the president would retain removal authority regardless of the JCS chairman's fixed term. They described how an unjustified replacement of the chairman could be politically costly to the president, and therefore the legislation sought to make it less controversial for a new president to replace the chairman by providing an "automatic opportunity" to do so in the first year of his administration. As bill cosponsor Senator Barry Goldwater (R-AZ) argued, giving the chief executive the chance to either reappoint the incumbent chairman or assign a new person to the role within the first nine months of a presidential term would "guarantee strong civilian control of a more influential Chairman of the Joint Chiefs of Staff."[61] While arguing for a new president to have a chance to appoint a new chairman in his first year, Levin also suggested that the removal of a chairman would otherwise be politically costly for a president: "the President's replacement of a Chairman which he, of course, may do at any time, becomes a highly political act in itself and subject to controversy."[62] Goldwater suggested that "practical considerations make it difficult for a President to actually dismiss a Chairman." At the same time, legislators recognized the president still had the authority to remove the JCS chairman at any point and that they were relying on the chief executive to choose not to take such an action. As Goldwater noted, "the law specifies that the Chairman 'serves at the pleasure of the President.'"[63]

Still, Congress reappraised its reliance on presidential self-restraint in relation to the JCS chairman several decades later. Whereas legislators in 1986 were eager to allow a new president an automatic opportunity to reconsider and potentially replace a chairman in the first year of his term, lawmakers in 2016 sought to reduce their reliance on self-restraint and err even more on the side of independence in professional military advice. They thus extended the length of the chairman and vice chairman terms from two years to four. The House Armed

---

[60] *Goldwater-Nichols Department of Defense Reorganization Act of 1986*, Conference Report, 115, 128.
[61] *Congressional Record*, 99th Congress, 2nd Session (September 16, 1986), 23547.
[62] *Congressional Record*, 99th Congress, 2nd Session (May 7, 1986), 9830.   [63] Ibid., 9804.

Services Committee report on the National Defense Authorization Act for Fiscal Year 2017 explained that the "committee believes that a longer term of office for the Chairman provides greater stability and continuity of military leadership at the Department of Defense."[64]

A related adjustment was to both stagger those terms and to state that, except for a presidential waiver, the vice chairman would not later be picked as chairman. As the House Armed Services Committee report explained, "by staggering the Chairman's term of office such that it is not aligned with the four-year presidential election cycle, the committee believes that the Chairman's role in providing independent military advice to the President and Secretary of Defense is reinforced."[65] Similarly, the Senate Armed Services Committee recommended "requir[ing] the Department of Defense to return to the staggered terms of service for the Chairman and Vice Chairman, which would prevent both officers from turning over at the same time, which has been the case since 2007 but was not as the law originally intended. The committee also recommends a provision that prohibits the Vice Chairman from being eligible to serve as the Chairman or any other position in the armed services." As the committee saw it, "this adjustment to the law would ensure a high quality of military advice to civilian leaders, and ultimately strengthen civilian control over the military."[66]

However, this new provision's dependence on self-restraint ended up being considerable. The law specified that the chairman would serve "a term of four years, beginning on October 1 of a year that is three years following a year evenly divisible by four." This meant that a president would not have an automatic opportunity to select a new chairman until more than halfway through his term.[67] Congress thus relied on the president to restrain himself by accepting this arrangement and not removing the JCS chairman prematurely in order to install someone of his own choosing.

3.2 Director of National Intelligence

In addressing intelligence failures preceding 9/11 (Zegart 2007), Congress again faced a dilemma about how to ensure the independence of a sensitive

---

[64] *National Defense Authorization Act for Fiscal Year 2017*, Report of the Committee on Armed Services, House of Representatives, 114th Congress, 2nd Session (Washington, DC: Government Printing Office, 2016), 206.

[65] Ibid., 206.

[66] *National Defense Authorization Act for Fiscal Year 2017*, Report to accompany S. 2943, Committee on Armed Services, United States Senate, 114th Congress, 2nd Session (Washington, DC: Government Printing Office, 2016), 242.

[67] *National Defense Authorization Act for Fiscal Year 2017*, Conference Report to accompany S. 2943, House of Representatives, 114th Congress, 2nd Session (Washington, DC: Government Printing Office, 2016), 355.

presidential appointment. Legislators sought to provide greater coordination of the intelligence community through the creation of the Office of the Director of National Intelligence in the Intelligence Reform and Terrorism Prevention Act of 2004. Simultaneously, they were also concerned with making sure that the DNI would not be subject to political pressure (Clark 2010; Xiao 2021). The tension between these two goals permeated debates over intelligence reform, and the legislative design – including an emphasis on qualifications for the position – assumed a degree of presidential self-restraint.

Throughout those debates, legislators and other advocates shared a belief that the DNI should be apolitical and objective. Senator Olympia Snowe (R-ME) wanted the DNI to "facilitate an atmosphere of objectivity, collectivity, [and] information sharing."[68] Likewise, Senator Daniel Akaka (D-HI) argued that "the DNI must be kept free of political pressures and independent of partisan policy agendas."[69] As Lee Hamilton, the vice chairman of the 9/11 Commission, stressed, "this question of independence is a genuine one. And we all know that politicalization [sic] of intelligence is a very, very difficult problem."[70]

Legislators particularly worried about the DNI's relationship with the president. As Senator Mary Landrieu (D-LA) stressed, "The DNI should not feel hamstrung to tell the President and other intelligence consumers what they want to hear; rather, the DNI must be able to tell them what they need to hear. The DNI must be independent and unsusceptible to the political whims of his/her superiors."[71] "A National Intelligence Director must not be a more powerful 'yes man' for the Administration in power," wrote Senator Carl Levin. "Our security depends on objective, independently arrived at intelligence."[72]

This concern led to a substantial focus on both the location of the DNI and its status within the executive branch. "The National Intelligence Director should not be in the Executive Office of the President or in the Cabinet," David Kay, a senior research fellow at the Potomac Institute for Policy Studies, testified in Senate hearings: "intelligence should not be part of the political apparatus or process."[73]

---

[68] *Intelligence Community Reform*, Hearing before the Select Committee on Intelligence of the United States Senate, 108th Congress, 2nd Session (Washington, DC: Government Printing Office, 2004), 34.

[69] *Congressional Record*, 108th Congress, 2nd Session (December 8, 2004), S11976.

[70] *The 9/11 Commission and Recommendations for the Future of Federal Law Enforcement and Border Security*, Hearing before the Committee on the Judiciary, United States Senate, 108th Congress, 2nd Session (Washington, DC: Government Printing Office, 2004), 46.

[71] *Congressional Record*, 108th Congress, 2nd Session (December 8, 2004), S11980.

[72] *National Intelligence Reform Act of 2004*, Report of the Committee on Governmental Affairs, United States Senate, 108th Congress, 2nd Session (Washington, DC: Government Printing Office, 2004), 92.

[73] *Reform of the United States Intelligence Community*, Hearings before the Select Committee on Intelligence, United States Senate, 108th Congress, 2nd Session (Washington, DC: Government Printing Office, 2005 [2004]), 21.

When Senator Levin asked him to elaborate on "that very vital point," Kay explained that a DNI "serves whoever is the President best by giving him the unvarnished truth, which will often not be welcomed."[74] In addition to specifying in the law that the DNI could not be in the Executive Office of the President, legislators also debated whether the DNI should be in the Cabinet. The final law did not specify Cabinet membership for the DNI, but it also did not explicitly forbid Cabinet status. "We do not say that this National Intelligence Director should be a Cabinet officer," stated Slade Gorton, another 9/11 commission member, "because we do think intelligence, the collection and communication of intelligence and operational planning should be separated from policy. Cabinet members are policymakers."[75] Advocates of Cabinet membership, such as Senator Dianne Feinstein (D-CA), viewed that status as providing the DNI with a "statutory and structural position of leadership."[76] But skeptics pushed back on this point. To Senator Jay Rockefeller (D-WV), the risk was that "if you put somebody in the Cabinet, there is ingrained throughout our history a sense of loyalty to the President of the United States." He suggested that Cabinet membership would involve "the loss of perceived independence."[77] "Most of us feel that we want to keep politics out of this equation," stated Senator Dick Durbin (D-IL). He worried about "creating a tension, between professionalism and political skills" in the DNI if they went "to a Cabinet-level position."[78]

While the DNI would not be located in the EOP and might not be a member of the Cabinet, other questions remained about how to ensure DNI independence. Some supporters of intelligence reform noted that it was also important for the DNI to have a good working relationship with the president. As Lee Hamilton testified, the 9/11 Commission envisioned a DNI that "serves at the pleasure of the President... he is the principal adviser to the President, and we think the importance of a good relationship between the President and the National Intelligence Director is crucial. So we say coterminous with the President."[79] Similarly, during floor debate, Senator Ted Stevens (R-AK) emphasized that the DNI was "not an elected official and is not directly accountable to the American people," meaning he would "only be able to be reined in by the President himself."[80]

But an exchange during Senate hearings on the legislation highlighted why that kind of political appointment could pose a problem. For the retired US Air Force

---

[74] Ibid., 75–76.
[75] *The 9/11 Commission and Recommendations for the Future of Federal Law Enforcement and Border Security*, Hearing, 46.
[76] *Intelligence Community Reform*, Hearing, 22.   [77] Ibid., 25.   [78] Ibid., 33.
[79] *The 9/11 Commission and Recommendations for the Future of Federal Law Enforcement and Border Security*, Hearing, 46.
[80] *Congressional Record*, 108th Congress, 2nd Session (December 8, 2004), S12003.

General Charles Boyd, a coterminous political appointment would compromise independence: "Those who serve at the pleasure of a President for an expected term limited to his, who comes to office precisely because of shared politics and political reliability, come, I should think, under enormous pressure or temptation to give the President what he wants rather than what he doesn't want, but needs." Boyd explained his concern over a lack of protections for the DNI: "When that servant is responsible for selecting the intelligence analysis to give his President, I think I'd prefer a professional to a political appointee with as much independence and job security as possible."[81] After Senator Levin described trying "to figure out if there are ways that we can promote that independence and that objectivity and that unvarnished opinion" and emphasized not placing the DNI in the EOP, Boyd replied enthusiastically: "I love what you just said. I think it is hugely important.... The coin of the realm ought to be his distance from the President, his independence of the President, his professionalism." Moreover, Boyd stressed that Congress could clearly state its expectations for the qualifications of a DNI by invoking the JCS chairman as a model: "You can write that legislation. You wrote it in the [1986] legislation that appoints the chairman of the Joint Chiefs. He's got to be a professional. You don't allow it otherwise.... There's a direct connection to being led by amateurs, having their analyses torqued to please a President's policy objectives."[82]

The final legislation would emphasize qualifications. As the law stated, "Any individual nominated for appointment as Director of National Intelligence shall have extensive national security expertise." In a provision noting that only one of the DNI and principal deputy DNI could potentially be a "commissioned officer in the Armed Forces in active status," the legislation stated that Congress felt it was "desirable" that either the DNI or the principal deputy DNI should be a commissioned officer or have experience with military intelligence.[83] And, of course, the DNI would also be subject to Senate consent, giving legislators the clear ability to impose a cost on the president for selecting a nominee they viewed as unqualified. But supporters of reform recognized they were relying on presidents to exercise good faith both in selecting a professional DNI and in not pressuring or firing that officeholder. As Hamilton put it, "You cannot ever remove the prospect of politicalization [sic] of intelligence, but you can decrease it."[84] While stressing that "the new Director cannot be seen as pursuing a political agenda of any kind or forcing the intelligence community to support

---

[81] *Reform of the United States Intelligence Community*, Hearings, 24.   [82] Ibid., 76–77.
[83] Intelligence Reform and Terrorism Prevention Act of 2004 (PL 108–458, 118 Stat. 3638, 3644, 3656, December 17, 2004).
[84] *The 9/11 Commission and Recommendations for the Future of Federal Law Enforcement and Border Security*, Hearing, 46.

a particular administration policy," Senator Rockefeller's follow-up also showed the dependence the arrangement had on presidential intentions: "I urge the President to nominate an individual to serve as the first Director of National Intelligence who embodies these qualifications."[85] In fact, Levin bemoaned the final legislation for not having enough statutory language to ensure independence: "When we wrote the Senate bill, we included provisions to promote the objectivity and independence of intelligence assessments and to provide a check on the new National Intelligence Director from becoming a policy or political arm of the White House. I am troubled that the conference report excludes some of those checks and significantly weakens others."[86] Once again, in legislation dealing with a sensitive appointment, Congress had addressed the tension between accountability and independence by relying on presidential self-restraint.

3.3 Federal Emergency Management Agency Administrator

The federal government's response to Hurricane Katrina in 2005 was widely viewed as botched, and in response, Congress faced the question of how to reform FEMA (Roberts 2006). Legislators grappled with how to balance ensuring qualified agency leadership with accountability and meaningful access to the president for that official. In passing the Post-Katrina Emergency Preparedness Reform Act of 2006 as part of appropriations legislation for the Department of Homeland Security (DHS), lawmakers looked to lessen their reliance on presidential self-restraint and ensure the president would choose an agency leader with relevant experience.[87] The new position of FEMA administrator (changed from director), established as a direct presidential adviser, remained subject to Senate consent and presidential removal. But Congress sought to narrow and guide the president's choice of nominee with new qualifications written into statute.

Several features of the law were aimed at reforming the agency. Many lawmakers placed an emphasis on the agency's location and status, intending to elevate its place within DHS. The senators who introduced the legislation, Susan Collins, Joseph Lieberman (D-CT), and Ken Salazar (D-CO), sought to respond to concerns about FEMA's status, which had changed after the agency had been folded into DHS under the Homeland Security Act of 2002. As David

---

[85] *Congressional Record*, 108th Congress, 2nd Session (December 8, 2004), S11959.
[86] Ibid., S11956.
[87] Jimmy Carter, "Federal Emergency Management Agency Message to the Congress Transmitting Reorganization Plan No. 3 of 1978," June 19, 1978, *The American Presidency Project*, www.presidency.ucsb.edu/documents/federal-emergency-management-agency-message-the-congress-transmitting-reorganization-plan.

Lewis (2008, 161–162) summarizes, this relocation had several effects, including the politicization of "an already appointee-laden agency by layering still more appointees on top of FEMA's existing management structure," a "mission-shift in the agency away from an all-hazards approach back to civil defense, particularly domestic terrorism," the "decreas[ing] prestige of FEMA jobs," and the need for FEMA "to compete for power and resources with other parts of DHS." Part of these senators' vision was to rebrand the agency. At one point, the idea was to call the agency "the National Preparedness and Response Authority (NPRA)."[88] The initially-introduced bill would have changed FEMA to the United States Emergency Management Authority. "US-EMA," Senator Collins said, would "signify a fresh start." This would also be part of their broader plan to "elevate US-EMA within DHS" and "protect it from departmental reorganizations."[89] While rebranding was abandoned, the final legislation emphasized FEMA's unique status within DHS. As Senator Lieberman explained, "we elevate FEMA to a special, independent status within the Department of Homeland Security much like what the Coast Guard and Secret Service now have – so that reorganizations could only occur by congressional action."[90]

Another feature intended to strengthen the agency was providing that the director would report directly to the president, rather than to the president through the DHS secretary. The hope was both to improve communication and to ensure the president would take expert advice in dealing with disasters. Advocates of this change invoked the JCS chairman – the president's principal military adviser – as a model. The investigative report of the Senate Committee on Homeland Security and Governmental Affairs suggested that the agency's director should "be assured of having sufficient access and clout by having the rank of Deputy Secretary [of DHS], and having a direct line of communication to the President during catastrophes. The Director would also serve as the Advisor to the President for national emergency management, in a manner akin to the Chairman of the Joint Chiefs of Staff." Similarly, Senators Daniel Akaka, Frank Lautenberg (D-NJ), and Mark Pryor (D-AR) advocated for the director to "have a direct – not a dotted – line to the President." They contrasted how former President Bill Clinton had "elevated the FEMA Director position to the Cabinet level" with what had occurred with the establishment of DHS: "the FEMA Director was reduced to the rank of

---

[88] *Hurricane Katrina: A Nation Still Unprepared*, Special Report of the Committee on Homeland Security and Governmental Affairs, S. Rept. 109–322, United States Senate, 109th Congress, 2nd Session (Washington, DC: Government Printing Office, 2006), 16.
[89] *Congressional Record*, 109th Congress, 2nd Session (July 25, 2006), 15661.
[90] *Congressional Record*, 109th Congress, 2nd Session (September 29, 2006), S10624.

Undersecretary requiring that he report to the Secretary of Homeland Security instead of the President."[91]

This emphasis on the director's relationship with the president was also part of the Senate hearings on the legislation. As Bruce Baughman, the president of the National Emergency Management Association, testified, just "as the Chairman of the Joint Chiefs has the direct reporting relationship with the President in times of war, so should the director of FEMA."[92] The final legislation stated directly that the "Administrator is the principal advisor to the President, the Homeland Security Council, and the [DHS] Secretary for all matters relating to emergency management in the United States." The administrator should present "the range of emergency preparedness, protection, response, recover, and mitigation options" for dealing with a particular situation. Inherently, then, the law sought to get the president to obtain and listen to expert advice. Finally, the statute stated that the president "may designate the Administrator to serve as a member of the Cabinet in the event of natural disasters, acts of terrorism, or other man-made disasters."[93]

However, the elevation of FEMA's leader to be a direct presidential adviser was not simply intended to provide the chief executive with more access to a key appointee or just to try to ensure the president would take that appointee's advice in dealing with emergencies. Congress also sought to improve the quality of that advice and to respond to a perceived problem of presidents not appointing qualified officials to run the agency. While Clinton's former FEMA Director James Lee Witt had been the first leader of the agency to have relevant experience in emergency management, this was unusual, not the norm. Those advocating changes to FEMA agreed that a primary problem during the administration of Republican President George W. Bush was a lack of appropriately qualified leadership. Neither the president's first FEMA director – Joseph Allbaugh, Bush's former chief of staff as Texas governor and 2000 campaign manager – nor the subsequent director – Michael Brown, an attorney and judges and stewards commissioner of the International Arabian Horse Association – had emergency management experience (Lewis 2008, 153–169).

The bipartisan report of the Senate Committee on Homeland Security and Governmental Affairs repeatedly emphasized the issue of qualifications. It asserted that "FEMA's former Director, Michael Brown, lacked the leadership

---

[91] *Hurricane Katrina*, Special Report, 16, 721–722.
[92] *One Year Later: Are We Prepared?* Hearing before a Subcommittee of the Committee on Appropriations, United States Senate, 109th Congress, 2nd Session (Washington, DC: Government Printing Office, 2007 [2006]), 51.
[93] *Congressional Record*, 109th Congress, 2nd Session (September 28, 2006), H7796.

skills that were needed" to tackle the crisis of Katrina. Though the report acknowledged "it is unclear that emergency-management experience alone is the single qualifier for senior leadership at FEMA," it stressed that "the leadership at the time of Katrina also lacked basic management experience and the leadership ability required to coordinate the entire federal government's response to a catastrophic event." The report focused on Brown's lack of relevant experience prior to his roles as general counsel, deputy director, and director of FEMA: "Prior to joining FEMA, Brown had little to no prior relevant emergency-management experience. Early in his career, he had some experience with municipal government, including municipal management, and had been a Commissioner for the International Arabian Horse Association for about 10 years."[94]

Moreover, the Committee identified this lack of relevant experience as a problem with Brown's entire leadership team. "With the exception of a FEMA employee who joined Brown's front office staff as Acting Director of Operations about a year after Brown became Under Secretary," the report noted, "none of the other individuals in the front office during the entire time he served as Under Secretary had any prior emergency-management experience." "The impact of having political [appointees] in the high ranks of FEMA ... that's what killed us," stated the former director of response at FEMA, Eric Tolbert (who left prior to Katrina): "in the senior ranks of FEMA there was nobody that even knew FEMA's history, much less understood the profession and the dynamics and the roles and responsibilities of the state and local governments." Even before Katrina, an examination of FEMA by a consulting firm had warned about a "lack of qualifications." Statements from senior FEMA executives claimed there was a "void" in agency leadership, that "none of the senior leadership understand the dynamics of how response and recovery actually works," and that the director's chief of staff, Patrick Rhode, "is purely political; he thinks White House."[95] Echoing these criticisms, Representative Tim Ryan (D-OH) described the agency as being run by incompetent political appointees: "the Republican appointed members of the emergency management system here in the United States of America, had five or six days, knowing that a hurricane was coming to the Gulf States, and we got the kind of response we got." Invoking Brown's lack of appropriate experience, he criticized the administration for having "appointed horse attorneys, equestrian attorneys to run FEMA."[96]

Reformers moved beyond such criticism and suggested the president would need statutory guidance to choose better agency leaders. Even as the initial bill

---

[94] *Hurricane Katrina*, Special Report, 6, 214. [95] Ibid., 214–215.
[96] *Congressional Record*, 109th Congress, 2nd Session (July 25, 2006), 15838–15839.

introduced by Senators Collins, Lieberman, and Salazar designated the administrator as the "principal emergency preparedness response advisor to the President," that direct access was tied to qualifications: "The Administrator shall have not less than 5 years of executive experience and management experience in the public or private sector, significant experience in crisis management or another relevant field, and a demonstrated ability to manage a substantial staff and budget."[97] The Senate report analyzing the failures surrounding Katrina explained the relevant experience lawmakers envisioned, stating that the administrator should "be selected from the ranks of professionals with experience in crisis management, in addition to substantial management and leadership experience, whether in the public, private, or non-profit sector." Elaborating on these qualifications, the report explained that "appropriate experience could include a military career with broad leadership experience; emergency-management experience and a proven track record of leading complex preparedness and response efforts; or private-sector experience successfully leading a company or organization through a crisis." Even those who disagreed with some of the report's conclusions agreed on the importance of qualified leadership. Senator George Voinovich (R-OH) suggested that "too much emphasis has been placed upon reconsidering the organizational structure of FEMA" and instead stressed that a "key to FEMA's effectiveness is ensuring the agency has capable and qualified leadership." Senator Carl Levin likewise emphasized that "FEMA needs to be strengthened" through "qualified leadership."[98]

In a Senate hearing on post-Katrina reform, witnesses also spoke of the need for more direct qualifications for senior FEMA roles. Baughman, the president of the National Emergency Management Association, told Congress that "there should be some recommended knowledge base established for the director of FEMA." His prepared statement elaborated that this should include "Emergency management or similar related career at the Federal, State or local government level," "Executive level management experience, governmental administration and budgeting," "Understanding of fundamental principles of population protection, disaster preparedness, mitigation, response and recovery, and command and control," "Understanding of the legislative process," and "Demonstrated leadership including the ability to exert authority and execute decisions in crisis situations." Similarly, Ellis Stanley, testifying for the

---

[97] "Post Katrina Emergency Management Reform Act of 2006," S. 3721, A Bill to amend the Homeland Security Act of 2002 to establish the United States Emergency Management Authority, and for other purposes, United States Senate, 109th Congress, 2nd Session (July 25, 2006), 13–14.

[98] *Hurricane Katrina*, Special Report, 16, 609, 701, 717.

International Association of Emergency Managers, asserted, "All the key leadership positions in FEMA need to be filled with experienced, qualified, knowledgeable personnel."[99]

Notably, Congress did not look to model the FEMA administrator off another position, the FBI director, which had a fixed term in office. This had been a recommendation of Baughman. He suggested that "a fixed term appointment for not less than 5 years should be considered, so the nomination is not political," which "would be similar to the model for the FBI Director." Moreover, Baughman had suggested another mechanism to try to ensure Congress's intent for the position's qualifications would be fulfilled, suggesting that "a vetting process should be established that includes a role for input by emergency management constituency groups similar to the American Bar Association in judicial nominations."[100]

The FEMA reforms were included in the final conference report of the appropriations legislation for DHS. The legislation made it clear that this was not to be an ordinary political appointee, specifying significant experience qualifications for the role. As the law stated, the administrator "shall be appointed from among individuals" with both "a demonstrated ability in and knowledge of emergency management and homeland security" and "not less than 5 years of executive leadership and management experience in the public or private sector." These specifications, while not as extensive as some reformers may have advocated, were comparable to the qualifications provided in statute for the JCS chairman.[101] Senator Lieberman stressed that the legislation balanced access to the president with relevant experience: "The FEMA Administrator will be the President's principal adviser in an emergency and the administrator and top regional officials will have to have appropriate experience and qualifications for the job."[102] Still, even with better-specified qualifications, advocates recognized that they were relying on the president to abide by those terms and on the Senate to impose a political cost otherwise. As Baughman had testified, the "President should continue to nominate and the Senate should continue to confirm the Director of FEMA," but "more Congressional consideration and scrutiny should be given to the nomination to ensure the appointed official meets established criteria."[103]

The FEMA legislation held out the promise of both encouraging the president to utilize expert advice for emergency management and pushing presidents to select more qualified administrators. Congress chose not to rely solely on the president to

---

[99] *One Year Later: Are We Prepared?* Hearing, 46, 51, 55.   [100] Ibid., 51.
[101] *Congressional Record*, 109th Congress, 2nd Session (September 28, 2006), H7796.
[102] *Congressional Record*, 109th Congress, 2nd Session (September 29, 2006), S10624.
[103] *One Year Later: Are We Prepared?* Hearing, 51.

choose a nominee with relevant experience. In fact, it specifically did not pass an alternative proposal by Rep. Mark Foley (R-FL), which would have avoided stipulating nomination qualifications because "the President has every right to name who he wants to [the position]."[104] However, President George W. Bush resisted those specifications even as he signed the legislation. "Section 503(c)(2) vests in the President authority to appoint the Administrator, by and with the advice and consent of the Senate," Bush's signing statement explained, "but purports to limit the qualifications of the pool of persons from whom the President may select the appointee in a manner that rules out a large portion of those persons best qualified by experience and knowledge to fill the office." Thus, the administration did not consider this to be a valid requirement under Article II's Appointments Clause: "The executive branch shall construe section 503(c)(2) in a manner consistent with the Appointments Clause of the Constitution." Similarly, Bush expressed concern over the law's description of how the administrator would provide advice to the president, executive branch officials, and Congress: "Section 503(c)(4) purports to regulate the provision of advice within the executive branch and to limit supervision of an executive branch official in the provision of advice to the Congress. The executive branch shall construe section 503(c)(4) in a manner consistent with the constitutional authority of the President to require the opinions of heads of departments and to supervise the unitary executive branch."[105] In response, Senators Collins, Lieberman, and Mary Landrieu wrote to Bush expressing concern about "the 'signing statement,' in which you express your intention to disregard provisions in the law intended to protect against further mistakes such as those that plagued the 2005 hurricane response."[106] The episode suggested again how formalistic understandings of the separation of powers could undermine Congress's efforts to rely less on presidential self-restraint.

4 Removal Reporting Requirements

4.1 Inspectors General

Debates about how to promote the independence of sensitive political appointments arose again in legislation addressing oversight of the executive branch, specifically the establishment and subsequent reform of inspectors general.

---

[104] Bryan Farrell, "FEMA Braces for Another Storm," *The Nation*, May 10, 2006, www.thenation.com/article/archive/fema-braces-another-storm/.

[105] George W. Bush, "Statement on Signing the Department of Homeland Security Appropriations Act, 2007," October 4, 2006, *The American Presidency Project*, www.presidency.ucsb.edu/documents/statement-signing-the-department-homeland-security-appropriations-act-2007.

[106] Shaun Waterman, "Analysis: FEMA Signing Statement Blasted," *UPI*, October 13, 2006, www.upi.com/Defense-News/2006/10/13/Analysis-FEMA-signing-statement-blasted/54451160739022/.

The Inspector General Act of 1978 followed on creations of IGs in the Departments of Health, Education, and Welfare in 1976 and Energy in 1977. The law's stated mission was "to promote economy, efficiency, and effectiveness," as well as "to provide a means for keeping the head of the establishment and the Congress fully and currently informed about problems and deficiencies" in the departments and agencies.[107] Lawmakers were interested in cleaning up "waste" in the bureaucracy. Beyond this objective, though, legislators would grapple with how to preserve the objectivity and neutrality of inspectors general in both its establishment of those offices in 1978 and in its 2008 reforms (Light 1993, chs. 3–4; Johnson & Newcomer 2020).

Legislators sought to safeguard IGs from political pressure while also making them accountable for their performance. IGs were meant to be able to investigate abuses within their departments and agencies and to communicate findings to Congress. Yet, in a post-Watergate context, thorny issues regarding their independence from the president emerged. Congress's solution was to write its expectations for presidential appointments of IGs into the statute, concerning both the nomination and removal of IGs. As in the JCS chairman, DNI, and FEMA administrator cases, a key part of Congress's choice was to set out qualifications for the position. As the statute stated, a president would be expected to nominate IGs, who would be subject to Senate confirmation, "without regard to political affiliation and solely on the basis of integrity and demonstrated ability in accounting, auditing, financial analysis, law, management analysis, public administration, or investigations." Additionally, Congress attempted to strengthen norms against politically-motivated dismissals through the use of removal reporting requirements. The law provided that an IG "may be removed from office by the President" but that "the President shall communicate the reasons for any such removal to both Houses of Congress."[108] The expectation of self-restraint was clear. Presidents were to avoid nominating overtly political officials for IGs, and the requirement to explain a removal was meant to discourage presidents from firing IGs without appropriate justification.

The legislation thus set up clear lines that the president was expected not to cross. IG independence would be promoted, asserted the Senate Committee on Governmental Affairs, "by taking the unusual step of requiring the President to report to Congress explaining his reasons for removing an incumbent of the office."[109] Representative L. H. Fountain (D-NC), the House sponsor of the

---

[107] Inspector General Act of 1978 (PL 95–452, 92 Stat. 1101, October 12, 1978).
[108] 92 Stat. 1101–1102.
[109] *Establishment of Offices of Inspector and Auditor General in Certain Executive Departments and Agencies*, Report of the Committee on Governmental Affairs, United States Senate, 95th Congress, 2nd Session, Report No. 95–1071 (Washington, DC: Government Printing Office, 1978), 9.

legislation, stressed the nomination criteria during floor debate before the act's passage: IGs would be "appointed by the President, subject to Senate confirmation, without regard to political affiliation and solely on the basis of integrity and demonstrated ability."[110] The Senate sponsor, Thomas Eagleton (D-MO), also expressed confidence during floor debate that the legislation would provide IGs "the requisite independence to carry out their broad mandates effectively." He pointed to the removal provision, stating that while an IG could be fired by a president, "the President must also communicate his reasons for doing so to the Congress."[111] An assumption behind this provision was that it would help raise the costs of an inappropriate IG removal.

Nevertheless, legislators wrestled with the reality that these institutional devices did not take away an inherent dependence on presidential self-restraint. Questions arose over whether the nomination and removal provisions would be sufficient to protect IG independence. William Medina, a designate for Assistant Secretary for Administration at the Department of Housing and Urban Development, argued in the House hearings on the legislation that "continuity of effort" for IGs was vital for them to complete their work. Too much turnover, he held, "would seriously impair the operation of a unit like this where investigations and audits carry over periods of time and across administrations." Thus, Medina posited that an IG should be a "career civil servant" position, rather than a presidential appointee. In response, Fountain argued that the legislation did not specifically call for a turnover in IGs across presidential administrations. He asked Medina if he was "aware of anything in this proposed legislation which would require or which you construe as intended to encourage the removal of an Inspector General whenever there is a change of administration," and he further stated, "I do not know of any language in the bill that does that." Medina again emphasized that the legislation "does make it a Presidential appointee." This led Fountain to speculate more about how the legislation might induce certain presidential behavior: "If he is not operating right and he is violating Presidential edicts, my guess is that the President would remove him, but it our intention that the President will appoint someone who will be able to remain there, and that it will be a nonpartisan appointment. . . . And I hope that it would be a civil servant from within the agency."[112]

For legislators, the choice to settle on institutional devices encouraging presidential self-restraint responded to potential constitutional concerns.

---

[110] *Congressional Record*, 95th Congress, 2nd Session (April 18, 1978), 10400.

[111] *Congressional Record*, 95th Congress, 2nd Session (September 22, 1978), 30952.

[112] *Establishment of Offices of Inspector General*, Hearings before a Subcommittee of the Committee on Government Operations, House of Representatives, 95th Congress, 1st Session (Washington, DC: Government Printing Office, 1977), 127.

Leaving the president with removal power would ensure that IGs were accountable, but it also would head off potential constitutional questions about the separation of powers. As Senator Eagleton asked, "How do we strike the proper balance?" Fountain explained some of his thinking in the Senate hearings on the legislation. An earlier draft of the legislation had included "a fixed term" and restricted the president's removal power over the IGs, but Fountain explained that "we were fearful of possible constitutional problems." Allowing the president "the power to remove the Inspector General" was important, Fountain reasoned, since "otherwise, if you happened to get an Inspector General who was not doing a competent job, you would have your hands tied." James Naughton, the counsel for the Intergovernmental Relations and Human Resources Subcommittee of the Committee on Government Operations, also explained, "we felt there really was a question as to whether an attempt to provide a fixed term with removal only by impeachment or some similar process might be construed by the courts as an unconstitutional restriction on the President's power of appointment." While "we would not have that problem if it were not a Presidential appointee," Naughton contended, "we felt it was important to have a Presidential appointee" for the role. Notably, Fountain admitted some of his reservations over this choice: "Weighing the pros and cons we finally concluded and agreed that a fixed term would not be necessary, although I personally was one who felt that we ought to have the assurance of the continuity of one man digging in year after year to clean these things up."[113]

The result was legislation that stated Congress's intent for IGs to be independent of presidential politics but that also relied significantly on presidents respecting the legislature's goal. IGs must "be totally independent and free from political pressure," Representative Frank Horton (R-NY) affirmed. "If I have any reservations at all," he nonetheless admitted, "they are concerned with that independence. I would merely suggest that we keep an eye on these IG's and see to it that they have the freedom to operate independently."[114]

However, just as Congress reconsidered its provisions for the independence of the JCS chairman decades later, legislators felt compelled to readdress aspects of the president's relationship to IGs. Part of the purpose of the Inspector General Reform Act of 2008 was to establish a Council of the Inspectors General on Economy and Efficiency and explicitly call for qualified appointments of additional IGs appointed by agency heads that were created as part of the Inspector General Amendments Act of 1988.[115] But lawmakers also expressed concerns that the 1978 law's removal reporting provisions had

---

[113] *Legislation to Establish Offices of Inspector General – H.R. 8588*, Hearings, 15–16.
[114] *Congressional Record*, 95th Congress, 2nd Session (April 18, 1978), 10404.
[115] Inspector General Act Amendments of 1988 (PL 100–504, 102 Stat. 2515, October 18, 1988).

been insufficient in dissuading presidents from undertaking unwarranted removals. Thus, they sought to strengthen the provision requiring the president to explain any removal of an IG. The 2008 statute amended the 1978 law by adding an advance-notice requirement: "If an Inspector General is removed from office or is transferred to another position or location within an establishment, the President shall communicate in writing the reasons for any such removal or transfer to both Houses of Congress, not later than 30 days before the removal or transfer."[116] Here too, Congress relied on the notion that reporting the reasons for IG removal would raise the cost to the president of doing so.

As in 1978, lawmakers repeatedly extolled the importance of independent IGs. "To effectively carry out their mission," explained Representative Edolphus Towns (D-NY), "Inspectors General must be independent and objective, which requires that they be insulated from improper management and political pressure."[117] "We all agree," stressed Representative Christopher Shays (R-CT), "that IGs should operate independently, free from political interference."[118]

But the perception for many legislators was that presidents had undermined this norm. Indeed, the fact that Congress was considering reform at all showed that lawmakers did not think that the 1978 law had bolstered a norm of self-restraint sufficiently. In the words of Representative Betty Sutton (D-OH), "politics has crept into the inner workings of the Inspectors General" and left "the door open for political pressure and influence to prejudice the job that they are supposed to perform." "Under President [George W.] Bush," Sutton elaborated, "only 18 percent of the Inspectors General have audit experience while 64 percent have political experience.... And what's more, over one-half of the IGs appointed by President Bush had made contributions to his campaign or to other Republicans candidates and over one-third had worked in a Republican White House prior to their appointment."[119] "Unfortunately, the appointment of Inspectors General has been both politicized and dumbed down," asserted Representative Jim Cooper (D-TN).[120] Eleanor Hill, a former IG at the Department of Defense, told lawmakers that, "while the statutory protections for independence are excellent, they are not foolproof. Not all IGs felt as secure

---

[116] Inspector General Reform Act of 2008 (PL 110–409, 122 Stat. 4302, October 14, 2008).
[117] *Inspectors General: Independence and Integrity*, Hearing before the Subcommittee on Government Management, Organization, and Procurement of the Committee on Oversight and Government Reform, House of Representatives, 110th Congress, 1st Session (Washington, DC: Government Printing Office, 2008 [2007]), 1.
[118] *Congressional Record*, 110th Congress, 2nd Session (September 25, 2008), H9881.
[119] *Congressional Record*, 110th Congress, 1st Session (October 3, 2007), H11183.
[120] *Inspectors General: Independence and Integrity*, Hearing, 4.

in their independence as I did."¹²¹ As the Senate Committee on Homeland Security and Governmental Affairs summed up, "time has revealed some shortcomings in the existing Act. It is essential that Inspectors General operate with sufficient independence to do their jobs well, yet the current IG structure does not go far enough to safeguard this independence."¹²²

One possible response to the perception that IGs were not sufficiently protected from political pressure and retaliation would have been to attempt to make them removable only for cause. Indeed, some lawmakers and witnesses viewed this as the clear answer. Phyllis Fong, an IG at the US Department of Agriculture, testified in a House hearing that an IG was "ultimately accountable to the President." Still, she explained, "the sense that I have from my colleagues in the community is that it would be very helpful to have some kind of protection so that IGs, when they take a position, have the understanding that they will not be removed tomorrow for a reason that may not be apparent, and so, in trying to develop proposals, we looked at terms, we looked at removal for cause."¹²³ "It seems like, at a bare minimum," averred Representative Cooper, "we have to put some sort of for-cause in there to protect IGs' independence."¹²⁴ Thus, the initial bill passed by the House would have combined the thirty-day notice provision with for-cause removal protections and a fixed seven-year term (Wilhelm 2024). "Our bill specifies that they may only be removed before the end of their term for permanent incapacity, inefficiency, neglect of duty, malfeasance or conviction of a felony, or conduct involving moral turpitude," Representative Sutton explained: "This takes the politics out of a position and a decision-making process where it never should have been in the first place." Moreover, "removal of an Inspector General must be communicated to both Houses of Congress at least 30 days before that inspector's removal."¹²⁵

Still, the idea of providing IGs with removal protections again raised constitutional questions. Congressional Research Service legislative attorney Vanessa Burrows provided supporters of removal protections with assurance that the provisions were constitutional: "According to the court, congressional restraints on the President's power of removal fall within the principle of separation of powers. In *Morrison* v. *Olson,* the Supreme Court expanded Congress' authority

---

[121] *Strengthening the Unique Role of the Nation's Inspectors General*, Hearing before the Committee on Homeland Security and Governmental Affairs, United States Senate, 110th Congress, 1st Session (Washington, DC: Government Printing Office, 2008 [2007]), 21.

[122] *Inspector General Reform Act of 2007*, Report of the Committee on Homeland Security and Governmental Affairs, United States Senate, 110th Congress, 2nd Session, Report 110–262 (Washington, DC: Government Printing Office, 2008), 1–2.

[123] *Inspectors General: Independence and Integrity*, Hearing, 40–42.   [124] Ibid., 117.

[125] *Congressional Record*, 110th Congress, 1st Session (October 3, 2007), H11183.

as established in *Humphrey's Executor.* The court held that now Congress has the authority to provide for-cause removal protection to any advice and consent officer."[126] By contrast, opponents of such provisions asserted that the House bill's removal protections were "likely unconstitutional." For Representative Pete Sessions (R-TX), the House bill's removal protections amounted to an "end-run... around [A]rticle II of the Constitution, which our Founding Fathers provided to the executive branch to ensure that all of our Nation['s] laws are faithfully executed." The inclusion of removal protections also led to objections and a veto threat from President George W. Bush: "The Administration strongly objects to this intrusion on the President's removal authority and his ability to hold IGs accountable for their performance. The responsibility to 'take Care that the Laws be faithfully executed' – which Article II vests solely in the President – includes the responsibility to supervise and guide how IGs and other executive branch officers investigate and respond to allegations of wrongdoing within the executive branch."[127]

Ultimately, the thirty-day advance-notice requirement was the primary change affecting the president's relationship with IGs. The Bush administration was more conciliatory to that stipulation. Clay Johnson, the deputy director of the Office of Management and Budget, said that it was a "generic statement" that "the President doesn't want any restrictions on his ability to appoint" an IG. He argued that "a term and specific reasons [for firing] would limit the ability to hold an IG accountable." By contrast, Johnson suggested that "some kind of a notification, I don't know whether it is 30 days, ..., but something like that might be appropriate."[128]

Lawmakers viewed this advance-notice requirement as significant. For Representative Henry Waxman (D-CA), the legislation "strengthens the good IGs by giving them greater independence," including requiring the president "to inform Congress 30 days before any IG is removed."[129] Senator Jon Kyl (R-AZ) described the provision as being "designed to allow Congress to respond to a situation where an inspector general is fired in order to impede his discovery of wrongdoing or for other improper reasons."[130] The "requirement that the President or appropriate agency head notify Congress 30 days before transferring

---

[126] *Inspectors General: Independence and Integrity,* Hearing, 98.
[127] George W. Bush, "Statement of Administration Policy: H.R. 928 – To Amend the Inspector General Act of 1978 to Enhance the Independence of the Inspectors General, to Create a Council of the Inspectors General on Integrity and Efficiency, and for Other Purposes," October 1, 2007, *The American Presidency Project,* www.presidency.ucsb.edu/documents/statement-administration-policy-hr-928-amend-the-inspector-general-act-1978-enhance-the.
[128] *Inspectors General: Independence and Integrity,* Hearing, 41.
[129] *Congressional Record,* 110th Congress, 2nd Session (September 25, 2008), H9882.
[130] *Congressional Record,* 110th Congress, 2nd Session (April 23, 2008), S3327.

or removing an Inspector General," the Senate Committee on Homeland Security and Governmental Affairs explained, "would allow for an appropriate dialogue with Congress in the event that the planned transfer or removal is viewed as an inappropriate or politically motivated attempt to terminate an effective Inspector General." This provision would require the administration "to supply written reasons for the planned transfer or termination," a device that "was widely endorsed by the IG community as a useful deterrent against improper intimidation or dismissal." Nonetheless, supporters admitted the thirty-day provision still relied on presidential self-restraint, encouraging the chief executive to not use his formal authority in ways contrary to congressional expectations. "While we hope that this advance notice will encourage useful communication between Congress and the Executive Branch on IG performance and serve as an effective deterrent against improper terminations," reported the Senate Committee, "we note that the provision does not alter the President's ultimate authorities with respect to Executive Branch employees."[131]

In 2022, Congress would elaborate on that requirement to provide a thirty-day notice and the "reasons" for an IG's removal in the National Defense Authorization Act for Fiscal Year 2023. It directed the president to provide the "substantive rationale, including detailed and case-specific reasons" for removal. It also narrowed the president's options for who could serve as an acting IG. The chair of the Council of the Inspectors General on Integrity and Efficiency, Allison Lerner, expressed "hope" that it would "prevent situations where IGs are removed for purely political reasons." Even with such reforms, however, Congress was ultimately relying on the president to exercise self-restraint and to avoid firing IGs, as opposed to enacting the for-cause removal protections that had been included in the PODA legislation.[132]

5 Caps

5.1 Senior Executive Service

Parallel to its efforts to crack down on perceived waste, fraud, and abuse in the administrative state after Watergate, Congress likewise sought to make the growing bureaucracy more manageable. "In light of Watergate," Senator Charles Percy (R-IL) stated, "I would think that we would want some way to discipline those Federal executives in the higher echelon of the Federal

---

[131] *Inspector General Reform Act of 2007*, Report, 4–5.
[132] Bob Bauer and Jack Goldsmith, "Inspector General Reform in the NDAA," *Lawfare*, December 23, 2022, www.lawfaremedia.org/article/inspector-general-reform-ndaa; *Safeguarding Inspector General Independence and Integrity*, Hearing before the Committee on Homeland Security and Governmental Affairs, United States Senate, 117th Congress, 1st Session (Washington, DC: Government Printing Office, 2022 [2021]), 10.

government."[133] A central question to this "disciplining" – across both parties – was what the proper level of political control within and of the administrative state ought to look like. "I think that during the Republican administrations, when we had Presidents who have tried to put some of their people into the proper positions, there has been a feeling on the Democratic side that that was wrong," Representative Trent Lott (R-MS) reflected: "Now when we have a Democrat administration, all of a sudden there is a need to open up the civil service a little bit and have the senior executives have an opportunity to have these higher positions. I think there is some danger here of further use of politics in these decisions. But we as Republicans, I think, have to rise above partisan politics ... and the more statesmanlike position is to try to get it done while we have a Democratic President."[134] Representative Mo Udall (D-AZ) suggested that holdovers from the administrations of Nixon and Republican President Gerald Ford "got themselves embedded. They are now dedicated career, loyal servants. They went in as political people to carry out the mandate of the Ford-Nixon administration. And then, as Jimmy Carter approached from Georgia with that army of people he was going to put in there to get his policies into effect, we suddenly found that these dedicated soldiers are career employees. We are going to bring all of this out in the open with this bill."[135]

That legislation, enacted as the Civil Service Reform Act of 1978, contained a new management corps, the Senior Executive Service (SES), that would function as a link between political appointees and civil servants. It comprised people rather than positions (Perry & Miller 1991). Talented managers would be able to access greater compensation than they otherwise would be eligible for in the civil service, and presidential administrations could more easily move officials within and across different agencies. The aim, according to Udall, was "to shake up this government and give managers the ability to manage."[136] But in the post-Watergate environment, lawmakers were worried about the potential of a president to utilize the new flexibility of the SES in ways they did not intend. As a result, they deployed another institutional device meant to bolster a norm of self-restraint: a cap. They instituted a percentage cap for how many SES positions could be filled by non-career officials both overall and at any given agency, while still encouraging the president to exercise self-restraint and stay well below that cap.

---

[133] *Civil Service Reform*, Hearings before the Committee on Government Affairs, Senate, 95th Congress, 2nd Session (Washington, DC: Government Printing Office, 1978), 898.
[134] *Congressional Record*, 95th Congress, 2nd Session (August 11, 1978), 25709.
[135] Ibid., 25710.
[136] "Congress Approves Civil Service Reforms," *CQ Almanac*, 34th ed. (1978), 818–835.

The possibilities of abuse of the SES system were not lost on lawmakers, particularly those opposing the legislation. Representative Newton Steers (R-MD) cautioned that "The Senior Executive Service strikes at the heart of the merit principle. It restores the spoils system we got rid of nearly a hundred years ago ... This bill, and its clear return to the spoils system, subjects our Federal work force to twin evils in the office of the Chief Executive: A clever knave or an honest blunderer." The bill was "fatally flawed" and would "open the door to politicization," charged Representative Herbert Harris (D-VA).[137] Representative Gladys Spellman suggested that the SES would be a mechanism for the president to fill the managerial ranks of the bureaucracy with political allies, arguing that the "SES was the one thing that struck terror in the hearts of civil servants."[138]

Still, many lawmakers felt that the president had a legitimate basis for wanting to install "their own people" into the service. For Representative Louis Stokes (D-OH), responsiveness to the president would "cause the Government to function more effectively."[139] Representative Joseph Fisher (D-VA) felt that the "top leadership" of the bureaucracy "should be chosen freely by the President and subject to change at every election."[140] As Health, Education, and Welfare Secretary Joseph Califano testified in a House hearing, "there is a tremendous difference between having, you know, [Nixon's chief of staff H.R.] Haldeman carry out your policy and having other people carry out your policy." Promoting bureaucratic performance would not require that "employees be insulated from being responsive to carrying out the laws, to following policies which change."[141]

At the same time, even supportive lawmakers took concerns about politicization seriously. They wrestled with this problem in debating the notion of a cap, specifically regarding how many political appointees an administration could install within the SES. The civil service reform bill mandated that no more than ten percent of the SES could comprise political appointees. Moreover, no more than 25 percent of SES officials within any agency could be political appointees, and the incorporation of SES personnel into an agency could not increase its proportion of political appointees.[142] But lawmakers still indicated their reliance on the president not to push his formal authority to the limits. As Senator Charles

---

[137] *Congressional Record*, 95th Congress, 2nd Session (August 11, 1978), 25724.
[138] Quoted in "Congress Approves Civil Service Reforms," *CQ Almanac* (1978).
[139] *Congressional Record*, 95th Congress, 2nd Session (September 13, 1978), 29271.
[140] Ibid., 19218.
[141] *Civil Service Reform*, Hearings before the Committee on Post Office and Civil Service, House of Representatives, 95th Congress, 2nd Session (Washington, DC: Government Printing Office, 1978), 69.
[142] Civil Service Reform Act of 1978 (PL 95–454, 92 Stat. 1111, 1159, October 13, 1978).

Mathias explained, "Ten percent should not become a goal of each administration." One of the aims of the legislation was, according to Mathias, "maximum utilization of career civil service employees." Congress's "hope" was that placement in the SES would "center on individual qualifications for Government service." While presidents were free to go up to the cap with their appointments, Mathias stressed that the "maximum placement of career employees will be in the best public interest."[143] Furthermore, the statute itself stated Congress's expectation that the administration would "appoint career executives to fill Senior Executive Service positions to the extent practicable."[144]

Thus, in expressing a hope that the president would avoid reaching the SES political appointee limits, Mathias had conceded that the legislation depended on presidential respect for Congress's intent for a qualified bureaucratic management corps. The institutional arrangement hinged on the expectation that presidents would restrain themselves from maximizing their ability to utilize political appointees rather than career executives.

5.2 Vacancies

The Federal Vacancies Reform Act of 1998 was passed in response to two congressional concerns. One problem was clarifying that all departments and agencies – unless specifically exempted – were subject to the rules of the existing vacancies statute. The Department of Justice (DOJ), in particular, had long argued that the original 1868 Vacancies Act did not apply to itself, since the department had been formally established in 1870. The result was a statute that clarified the applicability of Congress's vacancies rules. As Senator Robert Byrd explained, the DOJ's "intransigence" meant that it was "time for the [Congress] to state, in no uncertain terms, that no agency, none, not even the Justice Department, will be permitted to circumvent the Vacancies Act."[145] For Senator Strom Thurmond (R-SC), the risk was that if "Justice is not bound by the Act, the other departments are equally free to ignore it, as many of them do."[146]

But a second, broader problem that concerned Congress was the increasing number of "acting" appointees in the executive branch over time. Senator Byrd argued that "each time a vacancy is filled by an individual in violation of the Vacancies Act, yet another pebble is washed off the riverbank of the Senate's constitutional role, and that, as more and more of these pebbles

---

[143] *Congressional Record,* 95th Congress, 2nd Session (August 24, 1978), 27562.
[144] 92 Stat. 1155.
[145] *Oversight of the Implementation of the Vacancies Act,* Hearing before the Committee on Governmental Affairs, United States Senate, 105th Congress, 2nd Session (Washington, DC: Government Printing Office, 1998), 14.
[146] Ibid., 37.

tumble downstream, the bank weakens, until, finally, it collapses." Likewise, Senator Thurmond felt that acting appointments constituted an enduring and serious issue: "Recent Administrations, both Republican and Democrat, have failed to send nominations to the Senate in a timely manner. Instead, they have appointed people to serve in an acting capacity for long periods of time without seeking confirmation. This is a matter of great significance."[147] Senator Fred Thompson (R-TN) also emphasized that "the [Congressional Research Service] reports that 20 percent of all Presidential appointees are now acting." For Thompson, such an outcome was "clearly not what the Constitution envisioned" or "what the Congress envisioned." It amounted to an evasion of "the advice and consent powers of the Congress [that] are specifically set out in the Constitution."[148] Just as in the civil service legislation, Congress would address vacancies by utilizing a cap – in this case emphasizing time in service – as an institutional solution, a device that still significantly relied on presidential self-restraint.

Because lawmakers widely agreed that presidents were leaving too many positions vacant and relying too much on acting officials, they questioned whether the 120-day limit for an acting officer under the existing Vacancies Act was too long and subject to presidential abuse. As Senator Thompson ruefully observed, "it appears, ironically, that Congress by attempting to in some way delineate the way in which some of these appointments would be made and to really extend the time in which the President can make them – it started out 10 days and now it is up to 120 days – ... it has wound up divesting itself of its power because of the interpretation of these agencies."[149] For Senator Byrd, a time limit was vital to preventing presidential abuse. The "time restriction" is "the linchpin of this issue," he argued: "Without that barrier, without the 120-day limitation on the length of time a vacancy may be temporarily filled, no President, no President of either party or any party need ever, ever forward a nomination to the Senate." It would allow the president to "staff the Executive Branch with 'acting' officials who may occupy the vacant positions."[150] Byrd argued that stricter vacancies legislation was the key to protecting Congress and "the liberties of the people."[151]

While Congress criticized the president for leaving positions vacant and using acting officials, it nonetheless acknowledged its own role in perpetuating the problem. Legislators recognized that it simply took a long time for presidents to fill so many positions and for the Senate to confirm their nominees. While Senator Thurmond contended, "it was time to revitalize the Vacancies Act and make it

---

[147] *Congressional Record*, 105th Congress, 2nd Session (September 28, 1998), S11025, S11028.
[148] *Oversight of the Implementation of the Vacancies Act*, Hearing, 4–5.   [149] Ibid., 5.
[150] Ibid., 10.   [151] Ibid., 8.

relevant to the modern presidential appointments process," he admitted that Congress's previous solution of "extending the time for a nomination from 30 to 120 days has not solved the problem."[152] Along these lines, Senator Thompson acknowledged a seeming irony. Though 120 days already seemed "like an awful long time" for the president make relevant appointments, he nonetheless suggested that the sheer number of positions, combined with the requirement of Senate consent, necessitated increasing the length of time allowed for an acting appointment: "These appointments keep proliferating, and we know just the operation of the Executive Branch is getting harder because it is getting bigger all of the time. I think that is a bad trend. But if that is going to happen, we need more time."[153] Senator Dick Durbin alleged the Senate bore "some responsibility for this problem. If we do not move in a timely fashion to fill positions then we are certainly at least part of the problem."[154]

The concern about the difficulty of presidents filling so many positions involved a noteworthy assumption – the belief that presidents would want to fill political appointments. An exchange between public administration scholar Paul Light and Senator Thompson was revealing on this point. "There are simply too many top jobs in government, both career and political," Light testified before the Senate Governmental Affairs Committee. Thompson, however, was skeptical that presidents would be willing to reduce the number of political appointees: "What inducement is there going to be for any President to go along with an approach like this... does not every President want as many people as he can get in these Executive positions?" Light agreed, observing that "Presidents are convinced that more leaders equals more leadership, and it has been difficult to convince them otherwise."[155]

Without reducing the number of political appointees, legislators found themselves in a bind as to how to enforce vacancy rules. As Thompson observed, "Ultimately, the only sanction Congress has got is either the power of the purse or the power to hold up appointments." Byrd admitted that Congress was dependent to a significant degree on the president respecting statutory intent: "We cannot write a perfect law, and we cannot be blessed with Presidents who will always faithfully execute the laws. I am not saying that he is intentionally doing this any more than we, intentionally, have sat here and watched this happen without trying to do something about it."[156]

To a significant degree, then, the institutional device Congress chose – a longer cap on the time an acting official could serve – relied on the assumption that

---

[152] Ibid., 37.   [153] Ibid., 36.   [154] Ibid., 7.
[155] Ibid., 45–46. On the idea of reducing the number of political appointees, see Lewis (2008, 212–216).
[156] *Oversight of the Implementation of the Vacancies Act*, Hearing, 23–24.

presidents would want to fill vacant positions in the first place and would restrain themselves from either leaving them vacant or turning to acting officials instead. As the Senate Governmental Affairs Committee report on the legislation put it, the "enforcement mechanism" was "to make an office vacant if... no presidential nominee has been submitted to the Senate for the office." The Senate report declared that this update to the "Vacancies Act limits presidential authority to make acting appointments, while preserving the Senate's power to advise and consent."[157] Still, the legislation's inherent reliance on the president following Congress's wishes was also made clear in the report. It explained that "the vagaries of the vetting and nomination process now" made a longer cap of "150 days a more realistic time limit." In essence, the report described Congress as encouraging the president to respect legislative intent: "The Committee extends the time period for acting service so as to create an incentive for the President to submit a nomination. The submission of nominations also will lead to a reduction in the number of acting officials, a goal the Committee finds highly desirable."[158]

Indeed, the final legislation responded to the concerns over how many positions a president needed to fill, lengthening the time limit even further. In addition to clarifying the eligibility of acting officials – designating either "the first assistant to the office" or another person who had already received "the advice and consent of the Senate" to perform those functions – the law now stipulated that a person could serve as an acting officer for 210 days from the beginning of the vacancy. That individual could serve a further 210 days if the president made a nomination to the Senate, and a further 210 days if that nomination was rejected, withdrawn, or returned. Congress granted an even longer period for presidential transitions: the 210-day clock would not begin until 90 days after the president's inauguration, or after the date on which a vacancy occurred (O'Connell 2020, 625–637).[159]

Thus, Congress's hopes about presidential behavior were reflected in many of their statutory choices. A key assumption was that presidents would want to fill positions and avoid vacancies, but there were limits to Congress's ability to force the president to make a nomination. Even as he described the new limits on the use of acting officials in the law, Senator Byrd noted that the president might, "for whatever reason, fail to forward [a] nomination."[160] Second, the law assumed that presidents would not seek to exploit the longer limit on the

---

[157] *Federal Vacancies Reform Act of 1998*, Report of the Committee on Governmental Affairs, United States Senate, 105th Congress, 2nd Session, Report 105–250 (Washington, DC: Government Printing Office, 1998), 2, 5.
[158] Ibid., 13–14.
[159] Federal Vacancies Reform Act of 1998 (Section 151 of PL 105–277, 112 Stat. 2681–611, October 21, 1998).
[160] *Congressional Record*, 105th Congress, 2nd Session (October 21, 1998), S12824.

service of acting officials as a routine matter. But that time limit could potentially stretch to years if a president sought to strategically use the flexibility provided by the statute (Kinane 2021; Piper 2022). Vacancies reform may have had a cap, but it was one that still proved to rely significantly on the president's willingness to restrain himself.

6 Removal Protections

6.1 Social Security Administration Commissioner

When Congress decided that the Social Security Administration (SSA) needed reform, it again faced a dilemma of how to balance independence and accountability in redesigning its leadership structure. This law, however, is instructive as a contrast to the prior cases we have examined. Whereas our other cases detailed Congress adopting institutional solutions that in some way relied on presidential self-restraint, Congress selected an alternative for structuring the SSA that relied far less on these types of statutory expectations of presidential behavior than it could have. Similar to its provisions for the special counsel in the 1978 civil service legislation, Congress provided the SSA commissioner with for-cause removal protections, along with a fixed six-year term. Notably, these removal protections – the mechanism by which Congress sought to ensure independence without relying on self-restraint – came under constitutional scrutiny and would ultimately come undone through a combination of Supreme Court and presidential decisions. Thus, this case demonstrates how the rise of constitutional formalism can limit Congress's ability to avoid relying on presidential self-restraint in laws regarding presidential appointments.

Several aspects of the law were aimed at protecting SSA's independence. One feature was establishing SSA "as an independent agency," separated from its former institutional home, the Department of Health and Human Services (HHS). Another was the requirement that SSA's budget request be passed to Congress unrevised by the president; instead, it would be sent alongside the president's own budget request for SSA. Furthermore, the legislation created a seven-member advisory board with members selected by the president (with Senate consent), the Senate president pro tempore (based on advice from the chairman and ranking member of the Senate Finance Committee), and the House Speaker (based on advice from the chairman and ranking member of the House Ways and Means Committee). Those members would serve staggered six-year terms, and the board would be bipartisan.[161]

---

[161] *Social Security Administrative Reform Act of 1994*, Conference Report to accompany H.R. 4277, House of Representatives, 103rd Congress, 2nd Session (Washington, DC: Government Printing Office, 1994), 1, 6, 91–92.

The emphasis on independence also influenced Congress's consideration of how to change the agency's leadership structure. Lawmakers widely shared a desire to insulate the SSA from political pressure. Senate bill sponsor Daniel Patrick Moynihan (D-NY) argued for the need to "increase public confidence in Social Security by giving the agency more visibility and accountability, by improving administrative efficiency, and by insulating the agency from partisan politics." Likewise, Senator Donald Riegle (D-MI) advocated giving the agency "the independent standing that it ought to have." "We should be guided by the principle that we should do everything we can to organize and administer the social security program so that the public is justified in having a high degree of confidence in it," underscored Senator Chuck Grassley (R-IA): "Making the Social Security Administration an independent agency may help us do this."[162] The agency would be "walled off from political mischief," suggested Representative Toby Roth (R-WI), "to protect the hard-earned benefits of Social Security recipients."[163] "For too long the Social Security Administration has been caught in the middle of political and budgetary disputes," stated Representative J. J. Pickle (D-TX): "This legislation will go a long way to protecting the agency from the crossfire of partisan politics." Agency independence, posited Representative Bill Archer (R-TX), would "go a long way in making it less political, more responsive, and more accountable" and was "critical" for administering "the most important social program ever enacted." There would be "no more effective way to signify this program's importance," suggested House bill sponsor Representative Dan Rostenkowski (D-IL), "than to give SSA independent status."[164]

Beyond the consensus on the need to make SSA more independent, however, there was disagreement over how to structure the agency's leadership to achieve that goal. Lawmakers offered alternative proposals with institutional designs that differed in how much they relied on the president's willingness to allow SSA leadership to be independent in practice. The initial bill passed by the House relied far less on self-restraint by the president. House lawmakers sought to prevent the president from replacing the agency's leadership at will. In contrast to the prior arrangement in which the Commissioner of Social Security reported to the HHS Secretary, the House now sought to set up a three-member, bipartisan commission to lead the agency: "SSA would be governed by a three-member, full-time Board, appointed by the President with the advice and consent of the Senate to serve staggered, 6-year terms, with no more than two members being from the same

---

[162] *Establishing the Social Security Administration as an Independent Agency*, Hearing before the Committee on Finance, United States Senate, 103rd Congress, 1st Session (Washington, DC: Government Printing Office, 1994 [1993]), 51, 3, 49.

[163] *Congressional Record*, 103rd Congress, 2nd Session (May 17, 1994), 10565.

[164] *Congressional Record*, 103rd Congress, 2nd Session (August 11, 1994), 21522–21523.

political party." Importantly, the members would have for-cause removal protections: "Board members could be removed from office by the President only pursuant to a finding of neglect of duty or malfeasance in office." The Board would then appoint an executive director "to handle day-to-day operations," and that director "would be subject to removal from office before completion of his or her term only for cause found by the Board." This arrangement, the House report on the bill contended, was the best way to insulate the agency:

> The Committee believes that administration by an independent board would strengthen public confidence in the long-term viability of Social Security.... Further, the Committee regards the three separate requirements that apply to the Board – long, staggered terms; political balance among members; and removal of members based only on neglect of duty or malfeasance in office – as measures for insulating the Board from short-term political pressures and providing increased management stability.[165]

By contrast, another design alternative was more reliant on the president to restrain himself from firing the agency's leadership. Some advocated a single administrator for the agency. For example, a prior study by the 1983 Social Security Commission, headed by former Comptroller General Elmer Staats, had recommended a single administrator run the agency, with a part-time advisory board. Some House lawmakers hoped that alternative would prevail in conference with the Senate. Representative Jim Bunning (R-KY) noted he "would have preferred the form of administrative leadership structure specified in the bill I introduced in April of last year – a single Administrator supported by a seven-member part-time board instead of a three-member board as outlined in this bill." For Representative Archer, Bunning's preference was better because it "would establish the same form of leadership as was endorsed by the experts on the Staats panel."[166]

This was the route taken in the Senate bill. As Senator Moynihan explained, "Under [the Staats] proposal, SSA would be headed by a Commissioner to be appointed by the President with the advice and consent of the Senate. The bill also provided for a bipartisan, part-time advisory board to make recommendations on policy issues." In Senate hearings on the legislation, Staats explained the proposal's rationale:

> The panel concluded in favor of a single administrator, which when coupled with the advisory board of the type and with a charter which we have recommended, would provide in our opinion, a good balance between the

---

[165] *Social Security Administrative Reform Act of 1994*, Report to accompany H.R. 4277, House of Representatives, 103rd Congress, 2nd Session (Washington, DC: Government Printing Office, 1994), 52–54.
[166] *Congressional Record*, 103rd Congress, 2nd Session (May 17, 1994), 10563–10564.

need for a strong administrator responsible to the President, but with a board which would provide advice, assistance and protection for the integrity of the Social Security program.

The board itself would recommend candidates for the position of commissioner, which, Staats suggested, "would go a long way to toward assuring that a professional administrator is appointed to the position and the appointment of an individual who would be acceptable to both political parties." But at the same time, Staats emphasized that under the proposal for a single administrator subject to removal, the president would have significant responsibility for Social Security. "There is no way that you can remove the President from responsibility for a program of this size, magnitude and importance," Staats contended: "That means the President must take the responsibility for the appointment of the administrator." In fact, rather than trying to separate the position from the electoral calendar, Staats proposed aligning the term of the commissioner with the four-year term of the president: "We proposed that it be a 4-year term so that it be co-terminus with other presidents, to make it clear that the President did have this responsibility for administering the program." Eleanor Litwak, a member of the executive board of the National Council of Senior Citizens, disagreed with this approach, testifying that the "organization has long held that a bipartisan board with a fixed term remains the better guarantor against political manipulation."[167] But ultimately, the Senate passed the bill with a single administrator with "a term of 4 years coincident with the term of the President" and a seven-member, bipartisan advisory board with staggered terms.[168]

When the House and Senate conferees were reconciling the two bills, they were, in essence, deciding on how much authority they wanted the president to have over the SSA leadership and how dependent they would be on the president to not fire such leaders for political reasons. In the end, the compromise chosen was the least reliant on presidential self-restraint. The Senate bill's provision for a single administrator was combined with the House's emphasis on preventing arbitrary removals by the president. A single commissioner would be given a fixed six-year term and for-cause removal protections, and the agency would also have a bipartisan advisory board. As the conference report explained, Congress chose a single administrator to provide the agency with strong management: "In providing that a single administrator, rather than a bipartisan board, will head the independent agency, the conferees place high priority on management efficiency." At the same time, the conferees suggested that this structure would insulate the SSA commissioner from political pressure: "The conferees expect

---

[167] *Establishing the Social Security Administration as an Independent Agency*, Hearing, 51, 14–18, 37.
[168] *Congressional Record*, 103rd Congress, 2nd Session (May 23, 1994), 11342–11343.

that the key features of SSA's leadership structure as established in the conference agreement – i.e., independent status, a six-year term and the limitation on removal by the President, and a bipartisan advisory board – will be effective in assuring that policy errors resulting from inappropriate influence from outside the agency... do not recur in the future."[169]

This emphasis on stability and independence was also repeated in final debates on the legislation. Representative Bunning was "particularly pleased that the conferees chose to go along with this form of leadership for Social Security that I specified in my bill on the subject – a single administrator backed by a seven-member board." "In the past 17 years, 12 Commissioners or Acting Commissioners have come and gone," he explained, but the legislation "provides the kind of stability and a clear-cut line of responsibility any organization the size of SSA needs to be efficiently managed." Bunning stressed that the reform avoided a reliance on the president's good will toward the agency: "It emancipates the Social Security Administration from the bonds of politics and insulates it against the gale winds of Presidential posturing, bureaucratic infighting, and budgetary games." The law, Representative Eric Fingerhut (D-OH) stated, would "protect the agency from the political whims of the moment."[170]

The decision to provide the commission with removal protection, along with a fixed six-year term, was a striking example of Congress attempting to ensure the independence of a political appointee from the president. Relying less on presidential self-restraint, the law meant that the president's primary influence over the SSA would come through the nomination of a commissioner, subject to the consent of the Senate. But decades later, that choice would come undone under constitutional scrutiny from the Supreme Court and the president.

Indeed, in a preview of that outcome, Democratic President Bill Clinton noted some reservations upon signing the SSA legislation in 1994. The administration had changed its earlier stance opposing making SSA an independent agency and taking it out of HHS. "Distancing SSA from the Cabinet by establishing it as an independent agency would seriously dilute the attention and support it will receive at the highest level of our government," HHS Secretary Donna Shalala had previously told the Senate.[171] Now, Clinton embraced the law as "recogniz[ing] the program's importance by elevating the stature of the agency responsible for its administration." However, he also stated concern that the agency's leadership structure might be unconstitutional: "I must note that, in the opinion of the Department of Justice, the provision that

---

[169] *Social Security Administrative Reform Act of 1994*, Conference Report, 89–90.
[170] *Congressional Record*, 103rd Congress, 2nd Session (August 11, 1994), 21523–21525.
[171] *Establishing the Social Security Administration as an Independent Agency*, Hearing, 7.

the President can remove the single Commissioner only for neglect of duty or malfeasance in office raises a significant constitutional question." He suggested the need for "a corrective amendment that would resolve this constitutional question so as to eliminate the risk of litigation."[172] That innovation would indeed prove to be a vulnerability in the wake of later Supreme Court decisions, including over the leadership structure of the CFPB, the agency we discuss next.

6.2 Consumer Financial Protection Bureau Director

One of Congress's responses to the 2008 financial crisis and Great Recession was the creation of the CFPB as part of the Dodd-Frank Wall Street Reform and Consumer Protection Act of 2010. Just as in many of the other cases we have considered, Congress again faced a challenge of how to provide independence for a key appointee – the director of the new agency. But like the case of the SSA commissioner, this law is instructive as a contrast case. First, Congress relied less on expectations of presidential self-restraint, as legislators provided the director a five-year fixed term with removal protections. Second, the removal protections – the primary mechanism by which Congress sought to shield the director from political pressure – would later be struck down by the Supreme Court. The fate of that reform therefore demonstrates how constitutional formalism leaves Congress more reliant on presidential self-restraint in appointments.

Independence was central to every aspect of Congress's creation of CFPB. The legislation, which was supported almost exclusively by Democrats, would place the bureau in the Federal Reserve with an independent budget separated from the congressional appropriations process. This emphasis on independence also extended to the leadership of the agency. As Travis Plunkett, the legislative director of the Consumer Federation of America, argued, if the agency "is to be effective in its mission, it must be structured so that it is strong and independent with full authority to protect consumers."[173] Similarly, Senator Daniel Akaka envisioned an agency that would "be on the side of the consumer, that is independent, so the consumer is represented in the financial structure."[174] This independence, founding CFPB director Richard Cordray (2020, 30)

---

[172] William J. Clinton, "Statement on Signing the Social Security Independence and Program Improvements Act of 1994," August 15, 1994, *The American Presidency Project*, www.presidency.ucsb.edu/documents/statement-signing-the-social-security-independence-and-program-improvements-act-1994.

[173] *Creating a Consumer Financial Protection Agency: A Cornerstone of America's New Economic Foundation*, Hearing before the Committee on Banking, Housing, and Urban Affairs, United States Senate, 111th Congress, 1st Session (Washington, DC: Government Printing Office, 2010 [2009]), 94.

[174] *Congressional Record*, 111th Congress, 2nd Session (July 15, 2010), S5871.

would later write, was meant to insulate the agency "from the pressures" that the "banking lobbyists" would be able to "exert with their considerable influence over legislative and executive oversight." Likewise, Michael Barr, the Treasury Department Assistant Secretary for Financial Institutions who worked on the Obama administration's CFPB proposal, expressed confidence that "as long as there would be an independent budget, an independent director, independent policy making, and independent enforcement, you could put the agency on the moon and it wouldn't really matter."[175]

More generally, Democrats sought to protect the agency's leadership from political pressure imposed by a president. An earlier House version of the legislation would have protected the agency's independence by making it a commission, "changing it from [a proposed] agency headed by a single director to a commission headed by five commissioners," akin to the structure of other agencies like the Securities and Exchange Commission or the Federal Reserve Board of Governors.[176] There would be five commissioners with staggered terms and removal protections but no requirement for partisan balance. Asked by Representative John Dingell (D-MI) whether that structure would hurt the agency's "ability to be bi-partisan and limit any continuity that might arise out of shared leadership," Barr stated that "the focus" would instead be on choosing commissioners based "on expertise in the consumer financial marketplace, rather than be constrained by party affiliation."[177]

However, the Senate preferred a single director to a five-commissioner board (Kirsch & Mayer 2013, 85, 104–105). As a Senate report explained, the director would be protected from arbitrary presidential removal: "The Director is appointed by the President and confirmed by the Senate for a 5-year term and subject to removal for cause."[178] For supportive legislators, this change, along with the agency's unique location and funding structure, ensured the bureau's independence and effectiveness. "For the first time," Representative Carolyn Maloney (D-NY) underscored, "consumer protection authority will be housed in one place. It will be completely independent, with an independently appointed director, an independent budget, and an autonomous rulemaking

---

[175] Quoted in Kirsch & Mayer (2013, 90).

[176] *Consumer Financial Protection Agency Act of 2009*, Report to accompany H.R. 3126, House of Representatives, 111th Congress, 1st Session (Washington, DC: Government Printing Office, 2009), 98.

[177] *The Proposed Consumer Financial Protection Agency: Implications for Consumers and the FTC*, Hearing before the Subcommittee on Commerce, Trade, and Consumer Protection of the Committee on Energy and Commerce, House of Representatives, 111th Congress, 1st Session (Washington, DC: Government Printing Office, 2012 [2009]), 200.

[178] *The Restoring American Financial Stability Act of 2010*, Report to accompany S. 217, United States Senate, 111th Congress, 2nd Session, Report 111–176 (Washington, DC: Government Printing Office, 2010), 161.

authority." "Led by an independent director," echoed Representative Gregory Meeks (D-NY), "this office will be able to act swiftly so consumers will not need to wait for an act of Congress for years and years and years to receive protection from unscrupulous behavior."[179]

Supporters of the CFPB would further elaborate on the choice of an insulated single director in the face of subsequent Republican challenges and arguments in favor of changing the bureau to a commission structure. Soon after the legislation's enactment, Representative Sean Duffy (R-WI) asked Elizabeth Warren, then the Obama administration's special adviser to the Secretary of the Treasury for the CFPB, about the contrast between the CFPB structure and that of other independent commissions. Duffy expressed "concern that we are consolidating power in one person instead of a board." Though, as a law professor, she had proposed a commission structure for such an agency (Warren 2007), Warren testified that "having the single director when you have someone who is doing banking regulation makes for a more efficient operation."[180] In 2015, Warren again emphasized that a change from a single director to a commission "would just make the agency a weaker watchdog for consumers." Representative Barney Frank (D-MA), the House author of the 2010 law, stressed that he had "always been for a single director." And the Senate author, Chris Dodd (D-CT), stated that he was "strongly opposed" to attempts to change "the CFPB to a Commission, which would weaken the CFPB."[181]

Compared to most of the other cases we have examined, the choice to provide removal protections, combined with a five-year term, was one of the strongest efforts by Congress to ensure the independence of a political appointee from the president. This was a statute intended to rely less on presidential self-restraint, with the president's primary influence coming through the nomination of the director. Yet Congress's innovation in the CFPB structure later proved to be a vulnerability. In *Seila Law v. CFPB* (2020), the Supreme Court's conservative majority found that the for-cause protections for a single presidential appointee "violate[d] the separation of powers."[182] Supporters of the agency had viewed this leadership structure as "not unusual," comparable to "other banking regulators, such as the Federal Reserve Board of Governors, which has its own

---

[179] *Congressional Record*, 111th Congress, 2nd Session (June 30, 2010), H5239–H5240.

[180] *Oversight of the Consumer Financial Protection Bureau*, Hearing before the Subcommittee on Financial Institutions and Consumer Credit of the Committee on Financial Services, U.S. House of Representatives, 112th Congress, 1st Session (Washington, DC: Government Printing Office, 2011), 27.

[181] "Selected Quotes: Architects of Dodd-Frank Oppose a CFPB Commission Structure," Committee on Financial Services, U.S. House of Representatives, 2015, https://financialservices.house.gov/uploadedfiles/notable_quotes_cfpb_commission_structure.pdf.

[182] *Seila Law LLC v. Consumer Financial Protection Bureau*, 591 U.S. ___ (2020) (slip op., 11) (Roberts, C. J., opinion of the Court).

dedicated sources of funding and whose leaders, with fixed terms, are safe from being fired by the president for mere policy disagreements" (Cordray 2020, 30). But, committed to a more formalistic interpretation of Article II, the Court ensured that Congress was left more reliant on the president exercising self-restraint and respecting the CFPB's independence after all. Now even more dependent on the president's choice for director, the CFPB's structure ultimately "creat[ed] a feast or famine scenario for the agency's supporters and opponents" (SoRelle 2020, 205).

7 Conclusion

The preceding cases addressed the extent to which Congress has relied on presidents exercising self-restraint in their decisions about political appointees since the 1970s. Here, we briefly assess how recent political trends involving polarization, presidentialism, and constitutional formalism are affecting these types of statutes and impacting Congress's ability to restrain presidential power in the future.

7.1 Polarization and Presidentialism

To the extent that presidents do not always skirt Congress's efforts to establish norms surrounding certain political appointments, that is evidence of them exercising some degree of self-restraint. But to the extent that presidents skirt or even flout those expectations, that is evidence of them exploring how far they can push their power.

Of course, President Trump was not the first chief executive to test the limits of the statutes we have examined. For example, consider presidential actions toward IGs. Republican President Ronald Reagan dismissed all incumbent IGs on his first day in office, informing congressional leaders he had "exercised my power as President to remove" them.[183] The blanket termination led to bipartisan pushback and concern over politicizing the offices. Soon after, Reagan renominated several of the IGs (Light 1993, 102–105). His successor, Republican President George H. W. Bush, demanded the resignations of IGs, but he relented in the face of pushback from IGs and their defenders in Congress (Johnson & Newcomer 2020, 64). Concerns over politicization of IGs became so profound under President George W. Bush that Congress responded with the Inspector General Reform Act of 2008 (Johnson &

---

[183] Ronald Reagan, "Letter to the Speaker of the House and the President Pro Tempore of the Senate on the Inspector General Appointees of Certain Executive Agencies," *The American Presidency Project*, January 20, 1981, www.presidency.ucsb.edu/documents/letter-the-speaker-the-house-and-the-president-pro-tempore-the-senate-the-inspector.

Newcomer 2020, 76). Moreover, presidents have leveraged the flexibility offered by the caps in the SES and vacancies laws. Despite legislators hoping that presidents would avoid approaching the ten-percent overall cap on political appointees in the SES, chief executives of both parties – Bill Clinton, George W. Bush, Barack Obama, Donald Trump, and Joe Biden – all approached that ceiling during their administrations.[184] Similarly, lawmakers' hopes for a reduction in vacancies and the use of acting officials have gone unfulfilled during both Republican and Democratic administrations (Kinane 2021; Piper 2022). Congress's judgment in anticipating presidential conduct, then, has long been far from infallible.

That said, while presidents sometimes violated these statutory expectations, Donald Trump's first administration is especially instructive for its broad challenge to them. Trump's actions underscored how much Congress had relied on presidential self-restraint. Congress had sought to protect the independence of the FBI director in its 1976 legislation, and presidents had generally respected this norm of investigatory independence (Renan 2018, 2210). But fed up with the investigation into Russian interference in the 2016 election, Trump fired FBI Director James Comey with over six years left on his ten-year term (Skowronek et al. 2021, 81–83). Congress had emphasized inspector general independence in its 1978 and 2008 legislation. But Trump took on several IGs in his administration. Most pointedly, he fired the IG of the Intelligence Community, who had alerted Congress of the whistleblower report about Trump's withholding of military aid to Ukraine, an account that ultimately led to Trump's first impeachment (Skowronek et al. 2021, 187–188). Congress had expected the president to rely on the JCS chairman for independent counsel and to avoid politicizing the role. But Trump thrust JCS Chairman Mark Milley into a political firestorm, having him march alongside other administration officials after the forced clearing of Black Lives Matter protestors from Lafayette Square.[185] Congress had underscored the need for DNI independence when it created the position in 2004. But Trump grew impatient with his respected, independent DNI, former Senate Intelligence Committee member Dan Coats, and installed loyalists in the role in 2020 (Skowronek et al. 2021, 140–143). Congress had attempted to reduce vacancies and the use of acting officials with its 1998 legislation. But Trump left many positions vacant and enjoyed the "flexibility" afforded him by using acting officials, relying on

---

[184] Partnership for Public Service, "Senior Executive Service: Trends over 25 Years," July 2023, https://ourpublicservice.org/fed-figures/senior-executive-service-trends-over-25-years/.

[185] Michael Schaffer, "The Surreal Post-Trump Embrace of Mark Milley," *Politico Magazine*, March 24, 2023, www.politico.com/news/magazine/2023/03/24/mark-milley-lafayette-park-fallout-00088585.

them to carry out his policy goals to an unprecedented degree (Kinane n.d.).[186] Congress had stressed the independence of the OPM director and extolled the value of the civil service in its 1978 legislation. But late in his administration, Trump attempted to create a new Schedule F that would remove employees with a "policy-determining, policy-making, or policy-advocating character" from the competitive service, a move that would have stripped job protections from, at minimum, tens of thousands of career employees. He directed the acting appointee leading OPM to adopt regulations necessary for carrying out that executive order.[187]

In his second term, Trump quickly set about further challenging and defying these congressional expectations. Despite having appointed FBI Director Christopher Wray during his first administration, Trump's stated intention to remove Wray prior to the end of his ten-year term and to install a "staunch loyalist," Kash Patel, as a replacement led Wray to resign shortly before Trump took office again.[188] Trump fired JCS Chairman CQ Brown, Jr. before the completion of his four-year term and nominated a replacement who did not meet the qualifications specified in statute.[189] Reflecting his longstanding skepticism of the Intelligence Community, Trump chose former Representative Tulsi Gabbard, a top campaign surrogate with limited intelligence experience, to serve as DNI.[190] After Trump reinstated his executive order to allow him to "fire rogue bureaucrats," his acting OPM director moved to carry it out, sending guidance to federal agencies for determining which civil servants should be reclassified based on their "policy-making, policy-determining or policy-advocating" character.[191] The president undertook a mass firing of IGs without providing Congress with the

---

[186] Aaron Blake, "Trump's Government Full of Temps," *Washington Post*, February 21, 2020, www.washingtonpost.com/politics/2020/02/21/trump-has-had-an-acting-official-cabinet-level-job-1-out-every-9-days/. See also Skowronek et al. (2021, 137–152).

[187] Donald J. Trump, "Executive Order 13957—Creating Schedule F in the Excepted Service," October 21, 2020, *The American Presidency Project*, www.presidency.ucsb.edu/documents/executive-order-13957-creating-schedule-f-the-excepted-service. See also Moynihan (2022).

[188] Clare Foran and Morgan Rimmer, "Senate Confirms Kash Patel as Trump's FBI Director," *CNN*, February 20, 2025, www.cnn.com/2025/02/20/politics/senate-patel-confirmation-vote/index.html.

[189] Tara Copp and Lolita C. Baldor, "Trump Fires Chairman of the Joint Chiefs and Two Other Military Officers," *Associated Press*, February 21, 2025, www.apnews.com/article/trump-brown-joint-chiefs-of-staff-firing-fa428cc1508a583b3bf5e7a5a58f6acf.

[190] David Klepper, "Senate Confirms Gabbard as Trump's Director of National Intelligence after Republicans Fall in Line," *Associated Press*, February 12, 2025, www.apnews.com/article/tulsi-gabbard-trump-senate-national-intelligence-director-a1045b3f6bf91e491892e347b42cdc90.

[191] "Agenda47: President Trump's Plan to Dismantle the Deep State and Return Power to the American People," March 21, 2023, www.donaldjtrump.com/agenda47/agenda47-president-trumps-plan-to-dismantle-the-deep-state-and-return-power-to-the-american-people; Mimi Montgomery and Emily Peck, "Which Federal Workers Could Lose Protections under Trump Order," *Axios*, January 28, 2025, www.axios.com/local/washington-dc/2025/01/28/trump-executive-order-federal-workforce.

required thirty-day advance notice and substantive justification for their removal.[192] Furthermore, by moving to fire officials who had protections from at-will removal, such as the special counsel, the Trump administration has indicated its determination to challenge the constitutionality of such protections.[193]

The prospects for significant congressional pushback to such violations are attenuated by ascendant polarization. In what Frances Lee (2016) has termed an era of "insecure majorities," legislators have significant incentives to defend a co-partisan president rather than uphold the institutional prerogatives of Congress. Daryl Levinson and Richard Pildes (2006, 2011) have referred to this dynamic as a "separation of parties, not powers." As President Trump defied congressional expectations across these laws during his first term, he ultimately retained the support of his co-partisans. Even when Trump was impeached in the wake of the January 6 riot at the Capitol, in which the president's followers violently delayed certification of the 2020 election results, he overwhelmingly held on to Republican support.

Another major impact of rising polarization on political appointments and the dynamics of presidential self-restraint has been the so-called nuclear option. Senate Majority Leader Harry Reid's (D-NV) abolition in 2013 of the filibuster for all presidential nominees (except those to the Supreme Court) was a watershed development. While undertaken in response to Republican senators' resistance to President Obama's nominees, it also had significant implications for the politics of self-restraint.[194] Across our cases, lawmakers described how a president who fired an official for reasons at odds with a statute's expectations would face a political cost in the form of a tough Senate confirmation process for a replacement nominee. But by raising the threshold of senators necessary to thwart a new presidential nominee, the nuclear option diminished the potential cost of such a firing. As a result, some of those same statutes – such as the law addressing the FBI director – now rely even more on presidential self-restraint.

These dynamics are related to a bipartisan impulse to expand and utilize presidential power, elevating responsiveness to policy demands over structural constraints and norms. Though it is the conservative legal movement and Republican presidents who explicitly champion the unitary executive theory

---

[192] Sean Michael Newhouse, "Trump Fires Multiple Agency Inspectors General," *Government Executive*, January 25, 2025, www.govexec.com/oversight/2025/01/trump-fires-multiple-agency-inspectors-general/402504/.

[193] Josh Gerstein, "Trump's Power to Fire Executive Branch Officials Will Be Tested in Another Lawsuit," *Politico*, February 10, 2025, www.politico.com/news/2025/02/10/trump-executive-branch-lawsuit-00203354.

[194] Burgess Everett and Seung Min Kim, "Senate Goes for 'Nuclear Option,'" *Politico*, November 21, 2013, www.politico.com/story/2013/11/harry-reid-nuclear-option-100199.

(Skowronek 2009; Hollis-Brusky 2011; Howell & Moe 2023), Republicans and Democrats alike have turned to increased executive power in the half-century since Watergate. They have embraced what Elena Kagan (2001, 2245–2246) called "presidential administration," a system in which a president would make "the regulatory activity of the executive branch agencies into an extension of his own policy and political agenda." The project of institutionalizing regulatory review pushed by Republican Ronald Reagan was crystallized during Democrat Bill Clinton's administration as a core tenet of presidential power today (Ahmed, Menand, & Rosenblum 2024). In an analysis of regulatory review, James Blumstein (2001, 852) went so far as to contend that "it appears that we are all (or nearly all) Unitarians now." Furthermore, in their efforts to take control of the administrative state, presidents often turn to relying on loyal political appointees, even if that control can come at the expense of bureaucratic performance (Lewis 2008). And, amid congressional gridlock, presidents have increasingly embraced a politics of "catch-me-if-you-can," promising and pushing unilateral policy changes that are often cheered along by ideological allies in Congress (Orren & Skowronek 2017, 137–138). In a time of polarization, then, the attraction of turning to the executive for action is clear, and legacy-driven presidents are primed to stake their claims to authority rather than settle for inaction (Greenberg 2024).

On its own terms, the rise of presidentialism raises significant doubts about the potential for – and the practicability of – congressional expectations of presidential self-restraint. But when combined with another recent trend – the rise of constitutional formalism – fundamental questions about Congress's capacity to provide for independence in the executive branch emerge.

7.2 Constitutional Formalism

In several cases, we have noted that constitutional concerns were an influence on legislators to settle for institutional designs more reliant on presidential self-restraint. But the implications of more formalistic readings of the Constitution's separation of powers for the relationship between Congress and the presidency have only grown more profound in recent decades. The conservative legal movement's efforts on this front have culminated in the Supreme Court's embrace of a "juristocratic" understanding of the separation of powers, an interpretation by which courts can impose "limits on how Congress and the President may construct their interrelationships by statute" (Bowie & Renan 2022, 2020). As a practical matter, formalistic reasoning about the separation of powers has sharply curtailed Congress's ability to creatively address concerns about presidential power and has generally led to judicial decisions "limiting legislative power" (Bowie & Renan 2022, 2034). One development along these lines was a case that affected presidential power across many policymaking realms. When the Court invalidated the legislative veto – a device by which Congress could negate executive branch actions – in *INS v. Chadha* (1983), it closed off a way for Congress to grant presidents more policymaking authority without relying entirely on the chief executive's self-restraint and good intentions (Bowie & Renan 2022, 2118). That case's outcome subsequently affected policymaking in areas such as executive branch reorganization, war powers, and emergency powers.[195]

More recent decisions have directly affected appointments. As we noted in the discussion of the CFPB law, the Supreme Court's decision in *Seila Law v. Consumer Financial Protection Bureau* (2020) is an especially consequential case for the dynamics of congressional reliance versus non-reliance on presidential self-restraint. That decision invalidated the for-cause removal protections of the CFPB director, which had been a mechanism legislators used to try to augment the independence of that agency and to protect the director from political pressure. Whereas in the cases of the FBI director, JCS chairman, and OPM director, Congress had urged the president to exercise restraint and not to fire those officials before the conclusion of their respective fixed terms, Congress's decision to provide for-cause removal protections for the CFPB director (along with a five-year term in office) had been a choice to avoid relying on presidential self-restraint.

In *Seila Law*, the majority of justices chided Congress for attempting to provide the director with such insulation. "Instead of placing the agency under the leadership of a board with multiple members," Chief Justice John Roberts wrote in the majority opinion, "Congress provided that the CFPB would be led by a single Director, who serves for a longer term than the President and cannot be removed by the President except for inefficiency, neglect, or malfeasance." "Such an agency," the Court opined, "lacks a foundation in historical practice and clashes with constitutional structure by concentrating power in a unilateral actor insulated from Presidential control." The Court's decision endorsed the unitary executive theory: "Under our Constitution, the 'executive Power' – all of it – is 'vested in a President,' who must 'take Care that the Laws be faithfully executed,'" and held that, by implication, the director "must be removable by the President at will." Underscoring its formalistic understanding of Article II, the Court made clear that an insulated director "violates the separation of powers."[196]

---

[195] *INS v. Chadha*, 462 U.S. 919 (1983).
[196] *Seila Law LLC v. Consumer Financial Protection Bureau*, 591 U.S. __ (2020) (slip op., 1–3, 11) (Roberts, C. J., opinion of the Court).

The justices who dissented in *Seila Law* also recognized how the Court's decision constrained Congress's ability to structure the executive branch. In her dissenting opinion, Justice Elena Kagan argued that the Constitution "grants Congress authority to organize all of the institutions of American governance, provided only that those arrangements allow the President to perform his own constitutionally assigned duties." Kagan asserted that "the Court has commonly allowed those two branches to create zones of administrative independence by limiting the President's power to remove agency heads," and she emphasized that lawmakers had "wide leeway to limit the President's removal power in the interest of enhancing independence from politics in regulatory bodies like the CFPB." To Kagan, the Court's decision that the director's removal protections were invalid "wipes out a feature of that agency its creators thought fundamental to its mission – a measure of independence from political pressure."[197] In other words, the Court had taken away the ability of Congress to opt for an institutional arrangement that would avoid relying on the president's good will to allow the CFPB director to be independent.

In a subsequent case, *Collins v. Yellen* (2021), the Court applied its formalistic reasoning from *Seila Law* to rule that the single director of the Federal Housing Finance Administration (FHFA) could not have for-cause removal protections. The decision acknowledged that Congress, in passing the Housing and Economic Recovery Act of 2008, had intended for the FHFA's director to have a "5-year term" and be removable by the president only "for cause." But Justice Samuel Alito's majority opinion stated that the law's "for-cause restriction on the President's removal authority violates the separation of powers." Endorsing the unitary executive theory, Alito's opinion rejected the notion that Congress should be able to insulate the FHFA director from presidential control: "The removal power helps the President maintain a degree of control over the subordinates he needs to carry out his duties as the head of the Executive Branch."[198] The dissenting justices once again chided the Court majority for constraining Congress's ability to provide independence to officials in the executive branch. "In a line of decisions spanning more than half a century," Justice Sonia Sotomayor wrote, "this Court consistently approved of independent agencies and independent counsels within the Executive Branch.... In recent years, however, the Court has taken an unprecedentedly active role in policing Congress' decisions about which officers should enjoy independence." As Sotomayor saw it, the Court's constitutional formalism favored the president at the expense of Congress: "These decisions have focused almost exclusively on

---

[197] *Seila Law LLC v. Consumer Financial Protection Bureau*, 591 U.S. __ (2020) (slip op., 1, 4) (Kagan, J., dissenting).
[198] *Collins v. Yellen*, 594 U.S. __ (2021) (slip op. 4, 26–27) (Alito, J., opinion of the Court).

perceived threats to the separation of powers by limiting the President's removal power, while largely ignoring the Court's own encroachment on Congress' constitutional authority to structure the Executive Branch as it deems necessary."[199] By implication, then, the Court's formalism was preventing Congress from designing appointment legislation in a way that would be less reliant on presidential self-restraint.

The *Trump v. United States* (2024) case, which addressed whether President Trump should have immunity for his actions related to the January 6 riot at the Capitol and his contestation of the 2020 presidential election results, had even more significant ramifications for congressional authority. Finding that "the President is absolutely immune from criminal prosecution for conduct within his exclusive sphere of authority," the Court held that "Congress cannot – as a structural matter – regulate such actions, and courts cannot review them." Chief Justice Roberts's majority opinion explicitly applied this reasoning to the removal power: "the President's power to remove 'executive officers of the United States whom he has appointed' may not be regulated by Congress or reviewed by the courts."[200] In addition to stressing that Congress could not regulate the president's removal power over executive officers, Roberts offered a notable illustration in discussing the Justice Department.

Specifically, Roberts's opinion sharply challenged the norm of investigatory independence for the Justice Department. As Daphna Renan (2018, 2207) explains, this norm "insulates some types of prosecutorial and investigatory decisionmaking from the President," which is especially consequential for the president's relationship with the FBI director. Thus, it is a prime example of Congress relying on presidential self-restraint: expecting that the president would not seek to inappropriately pressure the FBI director or other DOJ officials to undertake certain investigations. But Roberts's opinion blasted through that norm and underscored that it truly was up to the president whether to follow it. As he wrote, the "President may discuss potential investigations and prosecutions with his Attorney General and other Justice Department officials to carry out his constitutional duty to 'take Care that the Laws be faithfully executed.'" Roberts further posited that a president's "threatened removal" of the attorney general "implicates 'conclusive and preclusive' Presidential authority," suggesting that the president's motive for firing a DOJ official could not be challenged.[201] In other words, the president's motive for removal did not matter.

---

[199] *Collins v. Yellen*, 594 U.S. __ (2021) (slip op., 4) (Sotomayor, J., dissenting).
[200] *Trump v. United States*, 603, U.S. __ (2024) (slip op., 20, 36) (Roberts, C. J., opinion of the Court).
[201] *Trump v. United States*, 603 U.S. __ (2024) (slip op., 20) (Roberts, C. J., opinion of the Court).

Just as in other cases, the dissenting justices described the Court's majority opinion as impacting Congress's ability to avoid a total reliance on presidential self-restraint and good will. Justice Sotomayor's dissent raised concerns that "any use of official power for any purpose, even the most corrupt purpose indicated by objective evidence of the most corrupt motives and intent, remains official and immune."[202] The implications of the decision for Congress's ability to proscribe criminal conduct by government officials, including the president, were noted by Justice Ketanji Brown Jackson in her dissent: "What is left in its wake is a greatly weakened Congress, which must stand idly by as the President disregards its criminal prohibitions and uses the powers of his office to push the envelope, while choosing to follow (or not) existing laws, as he sees fit."[203] As we noted in our Introduction, the Court's immunity decision also led President Joe Biden to state that the Court had established a "new principle" by which the only limits on the president's power would be "self-imposed."[204] In other words, the Court had left Congress – and the country – more reliant on a president's self-restraint.

Of course, presidential administrations have often advocated for judicial outcomes favoring executive power at the expense of Congress. The Reagan administration had pushed for the *Chadha* decision; the Trump administration had pursued the *Seila Law* case. But presidents have also extended the logic of these formalistic judicial decisions further. For example, the Biden administration's actions demonstrated how separation-of-powers formalism affects Congress's ability to rely less on presidential self-restraint in granting officials independence within the executive branch. Addressing the insulation of the SSA commissioner, the Biden administration – not the Court – made the critical move. When Biden fired the Trump-holdover commissioner prior to the end of his fixed term, the OLC invoked the formalist reasoning of the Supreme Court's recent decisions: "We think the best reading of *Collins* and *Seila Law* leads to the conclusion that, notwithstanding the statutory limitation on removal, the President can remove the SSA Commissioner at will." To be sure, the Biden administration was following a direction the Court had pointed. But the Biden OLC's opinion noted the concerns about the insulation of the commissioner that the Clinton OLC had raised, which had led to President Clinton issuing a skeptical signing statement in 1994. The Biden OLC opinion emphasized the president's own Article II authority: "the Constitution vests the executive

---

[202] *Trump v. United States*, 603 U.S. __ (2024) (slip op., 12) (Sotomayor, J., dissenting).
[203] *Trump v. United States*, 603 U.S. __ (2024) (slip op., 16) (Jackson, J., dissenting).
[204] Joseph R. Biden, "Remarks on the United States Supreme Court Ruling on Presidential Immunity," July 1, 2024, *The American Presidency Project*, www.presidency.ucsb.edu/documents/remarks-the-united-states-supreme-court-ruling-presidential-immunity.

power and other specific authorities in a President on whom it imposes a duty to 'take Care that the Laws be faithfully executed.'"²⁰⁵

Both the Court's decisions and that OLC opinion also had potential implications for the removal protections Congress provided for the Office of Special Counsel, headed by a single official insulated from at-will dismissal by the president. Both the *Collins v. Yellen* majority opinion and the OLC opinion specifically mentioned that the OSC was not being immediately addressed in those cases.²⁰⁶ But the specific reference to that agency suggested that the OSC could be vulnerable to a similar constitutional challenge, like the one the second Trump administration would raise.

Such decisions also pose challenges for future reforms Congress may debate involving appointments. For example, consider again the PODA legislation, which we discussed in our Introduction. Passed on a near party-line vote by House Democrats as a response to many of Trump's actions as president, the act proposed reforms to make it more difficult for a president to remove inspectors general, among many other objectives.²⁰⁷ But the Court's increasing constitutional formalism would likely challenge the legislature's ability to utilize such reforms (Bowie & Renan 2022).²⁰⁸ As we have pointed out, recent decisions demonstrate the conservative majority's skepticism of removal power protections for single officers (Dodds 2022), raising the significant possibility that the current Court would look unfavorably on removal protections for IGs.²⁰⁹ The implications of formalism for the president's removal powers would be difficult to counteract beyond attempting to increase political costs to the president through removal reporting requirements, as in the IG legislation. But the Court's decision that a president's motives do not matter in taking official actions, such as removals, would appear to dim Congress's hope that demanding the president's reasoning would serve as an effective check on dismissals.

Indeed, some justices on the Court have indicated that they would even forbid Congress from providing removal protections to commissioners at independent regulatory agencies. For example, in his concurring opinion in *Seila Law v. CFPB* (2020), Justice Clarence Thomas wrote, "with today's decision, the Court has repudiated almost every aspect of *Humphrey's Executor*," the 1935

---

²⁰⁵ "Constitutionality of the Commissioner of Social Security's Tenure Protection," Opinion of the Office of Legal Counsel, U.S. Department of Justice, July 8, 2021, 1, 3, 5.
²⁰⁶ *Collins v. Yellen* 594 U.S. __ (2021), 32, fn 21; "Constitutionality of the Commissioner of Social Security's Tenure Protection," OLC opinion, 15.
²⁰⁷ "Protecting Our Democracy Act: Section-by-Section," 2021, https://schiff.house.gov/imo/media/doc/PODA%20Section-by-Section%209.16.2021.pdf.
²⁰⁸ See also John A. Dearborn, Desmond S. King, and Stephen Skowronek, "How to Tame the Presidency after Trump," *New York Times*, March 16, 2021, www.nytimes.com/2021/03/16/opinion/congress-presidency-trump.html.
²⁰⁹ In addition to the cases discussed here, see also *Lucia v. SEC* (2018) and *U.S. v. Anthrex* (2021).

case in which the Court had held that the president could not remove an appointee to a "quasi-legislative" or "quasi-judicial" agency like an independent regulatory commission without cause. Thomas was determined to go further: "In a future case, I would repudiate what is left of this erroneous precedent."[210] If the Court were to embrace this level of separation-of-powers formalism, Congress would be left with little ability to provide for administrative insulation beyond bolstering norms of independence for officials and hoping the president goes along.

The cases reviewed here do offer another potential lesson on bolstering the norm of self-restraint. As suggested in the DNI, JCS chairman, and FEMA administrator cases, Congress might utilize stronger nomination criteria – such as stipulating past experience in particular types of roles – for particular appointments. Indeed, the JCS chairman and FEMA administrator positions, which provided more specific qualifications than did the law establishing the DNI, may be promising models. For example, Susan Hennessey and Benjamin Wittes suggest that the FEMA administrator guidelines could be a "model for other positions," such as "those with important responsibilities for public safety." They point to other instances of Congress indicating particular qualifications in appointments legislation, including provisions that the attorney general and solicitor general be "learned in the law" and the need for the "undersecretaries of energy for science and nuclear security" to "have 'extensive background' in their respective fields and be 'well-qualified to manage' the particular duties of their offices."[211]

Still, even here, there is a risk that constitutional formalism could undercut Congress's actions. The signing statement on the FEMA legislation issued by President George W. Bush, which questioned Congress's ability to impose qualification requirements for the director, is suggestive. It put forth a constitutional interpretation along the lines of a broader statement of formalistic skepticism that had been issued by assistant attorney general for the OLC, William Barr, during the George H. W. Bush administration. That opinion, entitled "Common Legislative Encroachments on Executive Branch Authority," suggested requiring the president to "nominate an official from among individuals named in lists submitted by the Speaker of the House and the President Pro Tempore of the Senate or other officers of Congress" was "an unconstitutional attempt to share in the appoint authority which is textually

---

[210] *Seila Law LLC v. Consumer Financial Protection Bureau*, 591 U.S. __ (2020) (slip op., 1) (Thomas, J., concurring); *Humphrey's Executor v. United States* 295 U.S. 602, 628 (1935).

[211] Susan Hennessey and Benjamin Wittes, "Hecukuva Job, Donnie!" *Foreign Policy*, September 14, 2017, https://foreignpolicy.com/2017/09/14/heckuva-job-donnie-fema-disaster-response/.

committed to the president alone." Moreover, the opinion suggested that "Congress also imposes impermissible qualifications requirements on principal officers," such as requiring that commissions have a specific number of commissioners "from a particular political party."[212]

Thus, this separation-of-powers formalism has revealed a developmental dilemma. It has raised the prospect of Congress being left more reliant on urging presidents to exercise self-restraint, even as a combination of presidentialism and polarization provides reasons to be concerned about presidential violations of legislators' statutory expectations. To be sure, tools such as fixed terms, removal reporting requirements, and nomination qualifications can help Congress indicate in its statutes firm preferences to insulate certain officials from political pressure and to advise the president to abide by those expectations. But ultimately, those tools are still institutional expressions of norms, and some degree of presidential buy-in is necessary to make them work (Renan 2018; Skowronek et al. 2021, 198). With constitutional formalism increasingly foreclosing the institutional remedies that involve less reliance on presidential self-restraint, it remains to be seen whether providing independence and insulation within the executive branch will remain an achievable goal for Congress.

---

[212] "Common Legislative Encroachments On Executive Branch Authority," Opinion of the Office of Legal Counsel, U.S. Department of Justice, July 27, 1989, 250.

References

Ahmed, Ashraf. 2022. "A Theory of Constitutional Norms." *Michigan Law Review* 120 (7): 1361–1418.

Ahmed, Ashraf, Lev Menand, and Noah A. Rosenblum. 2024. "The Making of Presidential Administration." *Harvard Law Review* 137 (8): 2131–221.

Alvis, J. David, Jeremy D. Bailey, and F. Flagg Taylor IV. 2013. *The Contested Removal Power, 1789–2010*. Lawrence, KS: University Press of Kansas.

Azari, Julia R., and Jennifer K. Smith. 2012. "Unwritten Rules: Informal Institutions in Established Democracies." *Perspectives on Politics* 10 (1): 37–55.

Ball, Terence, ed. 2003. *The Federalist*. New York: Cambridge University Press.

Blumstein, James F. 2001. "Regulatory Review by the Executive Office of the President: An Overview and Policy Analysis of Current Issues." *Duke Law Journal* 51 (3): 851–899.

Bolton, Alexander, and Sharece Thrower. 2022. *Checks in the Balance: Legislative Capacity and the Dynamics of Executive Power*. Princeton, NJ: Princeton University Press.

Bowie, Nikolas, and Daphna Renan. 2022. "The Separation-of-Powers Counterrevolution." *Yale Law Journal* 131 (7): 2020–2125.

Calabresi, Steven G., and Christopher S. Yoo. 2008. *The Unitary Executive: Presidential Power from Washington to Bush*. New Haven, CT: Yale University Press.

Clark, Lauren C. 2010. "Statutory Struggles of Administrative Agencies: The Director of National Intelligence and the CIA in a Post-9/11 World." *Administrative Law Review* 62 (2): 545–572.

Cordray, Richard. 2020. *Watchdog: How Protecting Consumers Can Save Our Families, Our Economy, and Our Democracy*. New York: Oxford University Press.

Dearborn, John A. 2021. *Power Shifts: Congress and Presidential Representation*. Chicago: University of Chicago Press.

Devins, Neal. 2009. "Presidential Unilateralism and Political Polarization: Why Today's Congress Lacks the Will and the Way to Stop Presidential Initiatives." *Willamette Law Review* 45 (3): 395–416.

Devins, Neal, and David E. Lewis. 2023. "The Independent Agency Myth." *Cornell Law Review* 108 (6): 1305–1374.

Dodds, Graham G. 2022. "Presidential Control of Independent Agencies' Leadership and Personnel: A Two-Case Study of Interbranch Contestation over the Bureaucracy and the Unitary Executive under Donald Trump." *Presidential Studies Quarterly* 52 (1): 168–194.

Epstein, David, and Sharyn O'Halloran. 1999. *Delegating Powers: A Transaction Cost Politics Approach to Policy Making under Separate Powers*. New York: Cambridge University Press.

Farrar-Myers, Victoria A. 2007. *Scripted for Change: The Institutionalization of the American Presidency*. College Station, TX: Texas A&M University Press.

Fiorina, Morris P. 1982. "Legislative Choice of Regulatory Forms: Legal Process or Administrative Process?" *Public Choice* 39 (1): 33–66.

Fisher, Louis. 2013. *Presidential War Power*, 3rd ed. Lawrence, KS: University Press of Kansas.

Gage, Beverly. 2022. *G-Man: J. Edgar Hoover and the Making of the American Century*. New York: Viking.

Gailmard, Sean, and John W. Patty. 2013. *Learning While Governing: Expertise and Accountability in the Executive Branch*. Chicago: University of Chicago Press.

Gerring, John. 2007. *Case Study Research. Principles and Practices*. New York: Cambridge University Press.

Greenberg, Jack B. 2024. "The Case for Agency: Three Dimensions of Discretion in Presidential Agenda Construction." *Presidential Studies Quarterly* 54 (3): 290–309.

Grove, Tara Leigh. 2020. "Presidential Laws and the Missing Interpretive Theory." *University of Pennsylvania Law Review* 168 (4): 877–930.

Hamlin, Leah A. 2019. "Qualified Tenure: Presidential Removal of the FBI Director." *Ohio Northern University Law Review* 44 (1): 55–84.

Hollis-Brusky, Amanda. 2011. "Helping Ideas Have Consequences: Political and Intellectual Investment in the Unitary Executive Theory, 1981–2000." *Denver University Law Review* 89 (1): 197–244.

Howell, William G., and Terry M. Moe. 2023. "The Strongman Presidency and the Two Logics of Presidential Power." *Presidential Studies Quarterly* 53 (2): 145–168.

Ingraham, Patricia W., and Carolyn Ban, eds. 1984. *Legislating Bureaucratic Change: The Civil Service Reform Act of 1978*. Albany, NY: State University of New York Press.

Johnson, Charles A., and Newcomer, Kathryn E. 2020. *U.S. Inspectors General: Truth Tellers in Turbulent Times*. Washington, DC: Brookings Institution Press.

Kagan, Elena. 2001. "Presidential Administration." *Harvard Law Review* 114 (8): 2245–2385.

Katz, Andrea Scoseria, and Noah A. Rosenblum. 2023. "Becoming the Administrator-in-Chief: *Myers* and the Progressive Presidency." *Columbia Law Review* 123 (8): 2153–2248.

Kinane, Christina M. 2021. "Control without Confirmation: The Politics of Vacancies in Presidential Appointments." *American Political Science Review* 115 (2): 599–614.

Kinane, Christina M. n.d. *Unconfirmed Power: Unilateral Governance at the Pleasure of the President*. Yale University, Working Manuscript.

Kirsch, Larry, and Robert N. Mayer. 2013. *Financial Justice: The People's Campaign to Stop Lender Abuse*. Santa Barbara, CA: Praeger.

LaPira, Timothy M., Lee Drutman, and Kevin R. Kosar, eds. 2020. *Congress Overwhelmed: The Decline in Congressional Capacity and Prospects for Reform*. Chicago: University of Chicago Press.

Lee, Frances E. 2016. *Insecure Majorities: Congress and the Perpetual Campaign*. Chicago: University of Chicago Press.

Levinson, Daryl J., and Richard H. Pildes. 2006. "Separation of Parties, Not Powers." *Harvard Law Review* 119 (8): 2311–2386.

Levitsky, Steven, and Daniel Ziblatt. 2018. *How Democracies Die*. New York: Crown Publishing Group.

Lewis, David E. 2003. *Presidents and the Politics of Agency Design: Political Insulation in the United States Government Bureaucracy, 1946–1997*. Stanford, CA: Stanford University Press.

Lewis, David E. 2008. *The Politics of Presidential Appointments: Political Control and Bureaucratic Performance*. Princeton, NJ: Princeton University Press.

Light, P. C. 1993. *Monitoring Government: Inspectors General and the Search for Accountability*. Washington, DC: Brookings Institution Press.

Lindsay, James M. 2003. "Deference and Defiance: The Shifting Rhythms of Executive- Legislative Relations in Foreign Policy." *Presidential Studies Quarterly* 33(3): 530–546.

McCarty, Nolan. 2004. "The Appointments Dilemma." *American Journal of Political Science* 48 (3): 413–428.

Moe, Terry M. 1989. "The Politics of Bureaucratic Structure." In *Can the Government Govern?* eds. John E. Chubb and Paul E. Peterson. Washington, DC: Brookings Institution Press, 267–329.

Moynihan, Donald P. 2004. "Protection Versus Flexibility: The Civil Service Reform Act, Competing Administrative Doctrines, and the Roots of Contemporary Public Management Debate." *Journal of Policy History* 16 (1): 1–33.

Moynihan, Donald P. 2022. "Public Management for Populists: Trump's Schedule F Executive Order and the Future of the Civil Service." *Public Administration Review* 82 (1): 174–178.

O'Connell, Anne Joseph. 2020. "Actings." *Columbia Law Review* 120 (3): 613–728.

Orren, Karen, and Stephen Skowronek. 2017. *The Policy State: An American Predicament.* Cambridge, MA: Harvard University Press.

Perry, James L., and Theodore K. Miller. 1991. "The Senior Executive Service: Is It Improving Managerial Performance?" *Public Administration Review* 51 (6): 554–563.

Piper, Christopher. 2022. "Presidential Strategy amidst the 'Broken' Appointments Process." *Presidential Studies Quarterly* 52 (4): 843–874.

Renan, Daphna. 2018. "Presidential Norms and Article II." *Harvard Law Review* 131 (8): 2187–2282.

Roberts, Patrick S. 2006. "FEMA and the Prospects for Reputation-Based Autonomy." *Studies in American Political Development* 20 (1): 57–87.

Schoenbrod, David. 1993. *Power without Responsibility: How Congress Abuses the People Through Delegation.* New Haven, CT: Yale University Press.

Skowronek, Stephen. 2009. "The Conservative Insurgency and Presidential Power: A Developmental Perspective on the Unitary Executive." *Harvard Law Review* 122 (8): 2070–2103.

Skowronek, Stephen, John A. Dearborn, and Desmond King. 2021. *Phantoms of a Beleaguered Republic: The Deep State and the Unitary Executive.* New York: Oxford University Press.

SoRelle, Mallory E. 2020. *Democracy Declined: The Failed Politics of Consumer Financial Protection.* Chicago: University of Chicago Press.

Warren, Elizabeth. 2007. "Unsafe at Any Rate." *Democracy* 5 (Summer): 8–19.

Wilhelm, Ben. 2024. "Removal of Inspectors General: Rules, Practice, and Considerations for Congress." *Congressional Research Service.* Report IF11546.

Wiseman, Alan E. 2009. "Delegation and Positive-Sum Bureaucracies." *Journal of Politics* 71 (3): 998–1014.

Xiao, Kevin. 2021. "Independence in Intelligence: National Security Reform after 9/11." Yale University, Working Paper.

Zegart, Amy B. 1999. *Flawed by Design: The Evolution of the CIA, JCS, and NSC.* Stanford, CA: Stanford University Press.

Zegart, Amy B. 2007. *Spying Blind: The CIA, the FBI, and the Origins of 9/11.* Princeton, NJ: Princeton University Press.

Acknowledgments

We are grateful to our shared adviser, Stephen Skowronek, for proposing that this intersection of our respective research agendas was worth taking up and for his advice throughout the project. For helpful questions, conversations, and feedback at various stages of the research-and-writing process, we thank Larry Bartels, Nicholas Bednar, Richard Bensel, Peter Bils, Sarah Binder, Alexander Bolton, Jesse Crosson, Matthew Eshbaugh-Soha, Kevin Evans, Jacob Hacker, Evan Haglund, Lucas Helms, Greg Huber, Christina Kinane, Maya Kornberg, George Krause, David Lewis, Robert Maranto, Lauren Mattioli, David Mayhew, Nolan McCarty, Bruce Oppenheimer, Rachel Potter, Andrew Reeves, Molly Reynolds, Leah Rosenstiel, Andrew Rudalevige, Jennifer Selin, Adam Sheingate, Steven B. Smith, Steven S. Smith, Ian Turner, Sharece Thrower, Joseph Warren, Alan Wiseman, and Charles Zug. We likewise appreciate series editor Frances Lee's belief in this project and her helpful guidance and advice throughout the publication process. We are deeply grateful as well for the generous and helpful comments from Cambridge University Press's anonymous reviewers, and to Sasirekha Sanjivi and Adam Hooper for shepherding the manuscript through production. Finally, for their patience and support throughout this project, we extend our absolute gratitude to Charlotte Blatt, Laura Hatchman, and Jacob Dearborn, and we dedicate this Element to them.

Cambridge Elements

American Politics

Frances E. Lee
Princeton University

Frances E. Lee is Professor of Politics at the Woodrow Wilson School of Princeton University. She is author of *Insecure Majorities: Congress and the Perpetual Campaign* (2016), *Beyond Ideology: Politics, Principles and Partisanship in the U.S. Senate* (2009), and coauthor of *Sizing Up the Senate: The Unequal Consequences of Equal Representation* (1999).

Advisory Board

Larry M. Bartels, *Vanderbilt University*
Marc Hetherington, *University of North Carolina at Chapel Hill*
Geoffrey C. Layman, *University of Notre Dame*
Suzanne Mettler, *Cornell University*
Hans Noel, *Georgetown University*
Eric Schickler, *University of California, Berkeley*
John Sides, *George Washington University*
Laura Stoker, *University of California, Berkeley*

About the Series

The Cambridge Elements Series in American Politics publishes authoritative contributions on American politics. Emphasizing works that address big, topical questions within the American political landscape, the series is open to all branches of the subfield and actively welcomes works that bridge subject domains. It publishes both original new research on topics likely to be of interest to a broad audience and state-of-the-art synthesis and reconsideration pieces that address salient questions and incorporate new data and cases to inform arguments.

Cambridge Elements

American Politics

Elements in the Series

The Study of US State Policy Diffusion: What Hath Walker Wrought?
Christopher Z. Mooney

Why Bad Policies Spread (and Good Ones Don't)
Charles R. Shipan and Craig Volden

The Partisan Next Door: Stereotypes of Party Supporters and Consequences for Polarization in America
Ethan C. Busby, Adam J. Howat, Jacob E. Rothschild and Richard M. Shafranek

The Dynamics of Public Opinion
Mary Layton Atkinson, K. Elizabeth Coggins, James A. Stimson and Frank R. Baumgartner

The Origins and Consequences of Congressional Party Election Agendas
Scott R. Meinke

The Full Armor of God: The Mobilization of Christian Nationalism in American Politics
Paul A. Djupe, Andrew R. Lewis and Anand E. Sokhey

The Dimensions and Implications of the Public's Reactions to the January 6, 2021, Invasion of the U.S. Capitol
Gary C. Jacobson

Cooperating Factions: A Network Analysis of Party Divisions in U.S Presidential Nominations
Rachel M. Blum, Hans C. Noel

The Haves and Have-Nots in Supreme Court Representation and Participation, 2016 to 2021
Kirsten Widner and Anna Gunderson

The Political Dynamics of Partisan Polarization
Eric R. Schmidt, Edward G. Carmines and Paul M. Sniderman

Shifting Allegiances: The Election of Latino Republicans to Congress and State Legislatures
Robert D. Alvarez and Jason P. Casellas

Congressional Expectations of Presidential Self-Restraint
Jack B. Greenberg and John A. Dearborn

A full series listing is available at: www.cambridge.org/EAMP

For EU product safety concerns, contact us at Calle de José Abascal, 56–1°, 28003 Madrid, Spain or eugpsr@cambridge.org.